7-68

THEY CAN LEARN ENGLISH

THEY CAN LEARN ENGLISH

Charlotte K. Brooks

American University

Wadsworth Publishing Company, Inc.
Belmont, California

Designer: Russell Leong
Cover illustration: Stephen Osborn

ISBN: 0-534-00188-2

L. C. Cat. Card No.: 72-81800

Printed in the United States of America

1 2 3 4 5 6 7 8 9 10—77 76 75 74 73

This book has been printed on recycled paper.

Preface

Still another book about teaching "those" children? Considering the plethora of material on how to reduce the outrageous percentage of children who fail in school, the question is inevitable. We are already drowning in discoveries about teaching methods, theories, descriptions of student behavior and learning patterns. But in all the wealth of this material, and there *is* a good deal of wealth in them, there seems to be a reluctance to get in and roll up the sleeves—to deal with the everyday problems of teachers and to suggest the practical but innovative and, most important, *successful* ways of doing what the theorists and researchers tell us needs to be done. We hear complaints, and as teachers, we couldn't agree more.

But what about the situation that is not a controlled research project, a funded experiment, a test situation? What about the daily, routine class situation—without the fanfare and glamour of "special" circumstances? What about the teacher who does not leave the program after six weeks or one semester, who is part of the school personnae—not an outsider preceded by an introduction to the assembly and living in transient headquarters on the other side of town?

Hopefully this book will provide guidelines for such teachers. The beginning teacher who is entering a world with more different kinds of people than he has met before. The master teacher who semester after semester watches his classroom fill with a different breed of students: the alienated, the uninvolved; those who are unhappy with the ways in which they have been learning English or tried to learn it in the past.

This book should also help people outside the teaching profession. Parents who are anxious to help their children but are unable to understand the specialized language of some methods books. College students who do not intend to teach but who sometimes tutor secondary school students and need a clearly understood source of practical principles and methods. Housewives, businessmen, and others who volunteer their free time for tutoring. Teacher's aides and paraprofessionals who are not always college—or even high school—graduates. Many of these people have found that dedication alone is not enough to help students; a book of practical teaching methods can be useful to them.

At one point in its development this book was to be titled *We Can Learn English*. It seemed to be a good idea because the book insists that teachers and students learn best together. "We" implies a cooperative learning venture between teacher and student made necessary because the English language continues to change, new writing styles continue to be introduced, instructional materials rapidly become obsolete and need replacement, and students as well as issues keep changing. But we decided on a title that needed less explanation, *They Can Learn English*, simply because it focuses precisely on the book's point of view: every student *can* learn forms of acceptable English if he is taught properly; every English teacher is responsible for learning how to teach effectively.

As Galileo said, we are all learners; there is no such thing as a teacher. Armed with the ability to ask the right questions, the teacher–learner and his students try to find answers. This book is the consequence of one teacher's efforts to include her students in her learning process.

Acknowledgments

Many, many people, in a number of ways, have contributed to the development of this book.

Dr. Hans Guth of California State College at San Jose made the initial suggestion that I do the book, and he has continued to advise in its production. Dr. Kenneth Goodman of Wayne State University and Dr. Mark Christiansen of the University of Tennessee gave considerable professional and personal assistance.

My sister, Mrs. Martha K. Cobb, and my aunts, Miss Odessa A. Moyse and Miss Hattie B. Kendrick, made specific contributions in research, writing, and criticism.

Members of my staff and teachers in the Department of English, District of Columbia Public Schools, developed some of the curricular materials used in this book; and many teachers and students in these and other schools have tried out the ideas expressed here. My superior officers in the school system have permitted me to take time off from my position to write.

Those students mentioned in the book—both in the United States and in England—helped me to know early in my teaching career how poorly prepared I was to teach them. Thus, indirectly, they helped me to write this book.

Friends and associates, personal as well as professional, have encouraged me. Most recently, Mrs. Toni Morrison, writer and editor, has helped in rewriting and editing this book.

Finally, my husband Walter, my son Joseph, and my mother Mrs. Ruby M. Kendrick have always believed in my ability to do such work and have given me the necessary freedom.

Contents

Introduction

Faust bartered his soul for another shot at the pleasures of youth. I think, sometimes, if I could arrange lower stakes, that I could be persuaded into some similar bargain for just a little segment of my youth. One year of it, in fact. My first year of teaching. It was, to the casual eye, a year laden with promise and laced with hope. With bright steps and a dazzled smile, I received my college diploma. The little scroll seemed to represent so much: it had been preceded by many courses in literature, months of student teaching in a vocational school, and the assurance of a job—a special kind of job. I was going to be a teacher. Like many graduates of liberal arts colleges, I had not thought seriously about teaching until my junior year, and the thoughts I did have were notable only for their naïveté. I expected to be teaching younger versions of myself: students who were able to read, eager to learn, anxious to stay in school, and determined to go on to college. Instead I had classes of boys and girls who read poorly or not at all; students who had learned to hate school; students who were bewildered and lost in school. They were black and I was black, but that didn't help. I couldn't understand why they resisted learning from me; why they didn't behave the way I expected and told them to; why, in short, they had so little respect for my great big diploma.

I wanted to quit. My frustration did for me what their frustration did for them: I made stupid mistakes, adopted defensive attitudes, refused to accept diverse points of view. I remember collecting knives from boys and insisting that they hand them to me handle first. It is a testimony to their generosity that they did it.

It would indeed gratify me to be able to teach that first year again. Whatever my later successes with students, that first year stands apart, separate and clear in its pain and sadness.

But bad as it was, it was not a total loss. My near despair forced me to invent workable methods; to create new ways of doing old things. I put a single word on the board; from it we built sentences; from those sentences we built other sentences and questions; from these sentences we developed stories. But nothing worked as well, even in that first confusing year, as my recognizing the need to know my students as separate human beings with differing life styles.

Describing my initial encounter with teaching—an encounter typical of our profession—is not a mere exercise in recall. It is because my experiences are so like those of many novice teachers that they are significant here. They pose an extremely important question: why did I have to discover so much alone? Why hadn't methods texts prepared me for my students? That was the question then, and that is the question now: why is there no simple, down-to-earth guide for new teachers going into schools where they will meet students from cultures unlike their own? Why is there no easily understandable book to help the teacher who, for years, may have had little success with such students, who may have been abruptly transferred into such a situation, or who may be seeing a cooperative, less demanding student body change into an inquiring, alienated one, placing enormous demands on the teacher?

In undertaking to write such a book, I made three major assumptions which formed the basis of my rationale.

The Rationale

1. Our *attitude* toward teaching is important. Students must be recognized as individual human beings with brains and hearts who can sense what our feelings about them are. Only an open and accepting attitude will earn their trust.

2. Our *expectations* for culturally different students should be high. We are not missionaries going among savages to civilize or patronize while anticipating failure. Nor are we prison guards whose main job is to keep students quiet with worthless busywork from which nothing is learned. We are teachers whose duty it is to make sure that each student discovers and applies his own best ways to learn. And we must expect that he can. When our confidence is high, so is the student's.

3. *Honesty* is vital. We must be honest with ourselves about our attitudes toward and expectations of these students. If we discover that we have unalterable prejudices about them, and recognize that these prejudices are crippling (to both the profession and the student), we should not teach them; we should seek another profession. For our hostilities (overt or covert) and our neglect (uninterested or benevolent) are quickly communicated to them. And the result can be devastating. If we respect, accept, and honor (love) these students, they will respect, accept, and honor (love) us as teachers. And they will learn from us.

An Overview

With those assumptions operating as a rationale, this book examines five major areas: language, literature, humanities, composition, and media. It deals first with what language is and how it develops among alienated students.

Ordinarily, work in language arts is considered the province of the elementary school. But to work with culturally diverse students, language arts ideas and skills are needed at all levels, for these students must be revealed to themselves as capable of learning how to listen to, speak, read, and write effectively all kinds of English. The more we know about language arts, the more we are able to differentiate among our students and identify the learning styles of each one. Work in language arts stems directly from an understanding and acceptance of varying styles. Although in actual practice language arts are integrated, this book discusses the separate skills (listening, speaking, writing, and reading) as well as the total discipline.

The language arts skills are followed by an examination of literature. Because it is so closely allied with reading, literature should always be a part of the English program, especially that of a culturally different or alienated student. Since literature need not always be read, we will explore the use of records and films. Nor is literature only the classics: we will consider adolescent literature, contemporary literature, and ways of teaching new poetry, biography, and other literary forms. Nor is literature separate from composition. We will also discuss ways of composing the short story, essay, poem, and film. Literature for a diverse student body must be multi-ethnic; this book examines effective ways to use black literature and the literatures of other minority groups. In every instance efforts have been made to show how literature can help the student see himself as an important and contributing human being, how it can encourage him to enjoy reading and composing, and how it can complement his language and language skills. (A complete list of all literary works mentioned in the text forms the bibliography at the end of this book.)

If a student sees himself as something less than a competent human being, he must be given a different view of himself and of his world. Humanities is frequently the means by which this change can be brought about. It is treated separately from literature in this book because humanities encompasses not only literature but other disciplines as well. Recognition that the student has many resources to bring to this kind of lesson is essential. In humanities as nowhere else, there is a real chance to use what the student knows—or can learn from his family and friends—in the realms of folklore, music, and art. Here is the chance to use the student's talent or bring to class the talents of people from the student's culture.

The chapter on composition is not confined to writing. Other creative compositional activities which can be devised for alienated students are suggested. Students with a history of writing failure need especially stimulating activities and should not be bound by conventional techniques in composition.

One chapter explores the exciting possibilities of using media in language classrooms.

A final chapter includes suggested lesson plans for each English area studied. Selected objectives or behavioral goals precede some plans, and specific approaches, methods, and assignments follow. Several of the suggested plans show how the areas of English can be effectively correlated for a culturally diverse population.

Each chapter mentions useful instructional materials, including books, audiovisual materials, inexpensive teaching aids, and other devices which teachers and students can make. Although particular textbooks in English are recommended for research and problem solving, it is wise to remember that most of these books have been written for the average student, and many of them are unsatisfactory for the student this book focuses on.

A Viewpoint about Learning

As mentioned earlier, in any classroom everyone is learning: teacher, students, lay readers, aides, paraprofessionals, technical assistants. And those associated with these people are learning also: parents, sisters and brothers, friends. They all learn from each other. As teachers—persons in charge—we must devise strategies to find out what all these people know and find ways to help them share their knowledge.

It is also true that in any classroom everyone is a teacher; therefore we must devise opportunities that will permit everybody to teach everybody else. To effect this mutual learning situation, we might employ what can be called the D.T.A., or Dumb Teacher Approach. Dumb, of course, has two major meanings: "silent" and "stupid." Here we mean both.

As teachers, we have been lectured quite a lot. In high school and college, we became accustomed to this barrage of information. Our teachers were not "dumb" in the sense of being silent. They were highly verbal and even loquacious. But what I recommend is that you deliberately assume a "dumb" posture; that is, try to remain silent and try *not* to be a know-it-all, the unchallenged source of all knowledge, the civilized, omniscient dispenser of what should be learned. We must admit that we really don't know everything and that our students know more than we do about many things. We must let them teach us as well as each other.

Most of what I know about the D.T.A. comes from teaching a year in a modern secondary school in Birmingham, England. This school, the Dame Elizabeth Cadbury School, teaches both boys and girls aged 11 to 15. I started my D.T.A. by pronouncing the city as though it were in Alabama; I was told to say Birmingh'm.

When I entered my form (classroom), the students stood and stood and stood and stood. Finally a girl, who later became my monitor (really my teacher), whispered to me, "Miss, they'll keep on standing until you *tell* them to sit." Sure enough, they sat when I told them to.

I asked for thumbtacks and found that I should have requested drawing pins.

I wanted a trash basket and learned about litter bins and dust bins.

I said "learned" and "burned"; then changed to "learnt" and "burnt."
I asked my students to put periods at the ends of sentences, and *learnt*
that I should have asked for full stops.

I taught them to put colons after the salutations of business letters, and
they taught me to use commas.

I stopped writing "color" and "labor" and "specialty" and "jewelry," and
wrote "colour" and "labour" and "speciality" and "jewellery." (And I pronounced every syllable in "speciality.")

I found out that I must not say "bloody" or "khaki" or "bum"—and
several other words. In short, I discovered that I could learn from students
as well as teach them.

I learned from my students to write, to spell, to talk, and to act in a
different way, but I did it without relinquishing my American ways of writing
and spelling and talking and acting. After a year in England I would return
to teaching in the United States and would have to go back to American
English.

What I learned was more profound than these superficial changes suggest.
I learned that I was different but—because I was a confident adult—in no way
inferior. I was willing and anxious to learn new ways, and my students were
willing and anxious to teach me. But I taught them my ways also, and I think
they were willing to learn primarily because they clearly saw how willing I
was to learn from them.

The D.T.A. is a useful way to develop a creative mutual learning experience.

And perhaps that is the most important point. Everything in the world
has something to do with teaching English; if we are to work with the many
different kinds of students who are not now learning English well, we must
begin to comprehend differences without judging students as inferior *because*
they are different. We must use what students already know to help them to
discover what they can do.

They *can* learn English.

Let's Face It

However extensive our preparation, however deep our commitment, we
will not always be successful. No teacher ever is. We may work out magnificent
plans, we may learn as much as possible about our students—about their
resources and strengths and weaknesses—but instant success is not inevitable.

John Holt, Jonathan Kozol, and others have recorded some of their
failures. Let me tell you about some of mine.

Once, rather early in my teaching career, I taught a sensitive, intelligent
young boy. I was still teaching quite a lot of meaningless, repetitive grammar,
and had no real knowledge of what my students had "had" in elementary

school. One day I punished the class for something I considered terrible at the time and had them write over and over about their misdeeds. Teachers still do this, and I can't think of a better way to turn students against writing. The sensitive young boy had been absent, and when he came in and saw what the class was doing, he said simply—and sensibly—"This is silly."

I was furious. Yes, I was tired and overworked, but that was no excuse for what followed. I took the youngster to my room and had a "talk" with him. I berated him and sent him home in tears. I compounded a silly punishment with a destructive one.

Recently I saw a young woman who had been in a seventh grade class I taught some years ago. She was in the class a short time, but that time coincided with my concentration on diagramming sentences. Unfortunately, she left with her mother for Africa before we really got into composition; before I discovered how evocative the phrase "I wish I were . . ." could be; before I began using magazine covers to elicit ideas; and before we had a "happening," which did not go by that name then but was simply called a hobby show. She left before any of our exciting discoveries in human relations.

When she saw me, she said, "Oh, Mrs. Brooks, I've never forgotten that dull diagramming we did in your English class." That's all she remembered. It served me right.

I remember far too much dependence on supervisors and curriculum guides and textbooks, and too little faith in myself and in my students. For far too long, I trusted test results and often grouped my students, as my administrators did, on what I now know were the results of false or misleading IQ, reading, and other verbal tests. If we were to believe most of these tests today, we would say that our urban and rural areas are full of stupid, retarded people, incapable of learning much. Patently untrue.

The point is that we can learn as much from our mistakes as from our successes, probably more if we are honest. So, before reading any further in this book, think back—as far back as you can—in your school career, and ask yourself these questions about your experiences in language arts and English.

What was your first day in school like? Happy or unhappy? Why?

Did you learn to read in school or before? Were your experiences with reading good or bad? Why?

Was your language acceptable when you entered school? Did this have any influence on your learning?

In elementary school, can you remember any specific experiences in listening, speaking, reading, or writing that were important to you? How have they influenced you?

Did an early school experience or a later one interest you in entering the field of English? Describe it. If not, why did you enter this field?

Recall some very bad or very good teaching you had in English. Analyze it and identify what was wrong or right.

There are probably other questions which are more directly applicable to your experiences. Think about them and, as you read this book, relate what you read to your experiences or to the experiences of others.

And then remember that, despite some rather terrible experiences, you did learn, and learn to love, English. So can your students—whatever their background.

1

Who Are "They"?

Father, Mother, and Me,
Sister, and Auntie say
All the people like us are We;
Everyone else is They.

The third person plural pronoun is really a simple word. It has an uncomplex function and no derogatory or euphemistic connotation. Despite its innocuousness, the word has become a way to both acknowledge and deny a distance, a separateness, between teachers and students. It may have been safe, even necessary at one time, to construct such barriers of distance, but it is no longer possible to maintain them without seriously endangering the emotional and intellectual lives of those we teach. Many of us sometimes inject a negative element into the word "they" when we refer to students: "What do *they* want?" "Why can't *they* learn?" Although it is natural to use the word when referring to persons who are not *us,* and persons who are not *like us,* we frequently and unconsciously extend the meaning to include those whose differences are unacceptable to us.

One way to decrease the distance that may exist between ourselves and our students, and to take the contempt (overt or covert) from the word, is to discover who "they" are.

"They" Are JoAnn

There are too many windowpanes out of the house, too many cracks in the floor, and too many people running in and out for JoAnn to bathe behind the heater propped up by a block of wood. JoAnn often smells bad. Her father is an old man, too old for work, too young for a pension. Her mother died young after bearing too many babies. In her secondary school, JoAnn can learn more in three days than the other students who come every day. JoAnn calls them "dummies." Reading comes easily to her, and some books are even good enough to be interesting. Spelling is fun: you just listen to the sounds and write—usually—what you hear. The other stuff can be learned at one sitting, so why go to school and be bored? Anyway, the teachers are always bothering you about bringing money to buy books. Books are not free in JoAnn's public school. The little "hinkty" kids don't let you look in their books, and the poor ones are like JoAnn: they have no books.

A special note goes with JoAnn when she is promoted from elementary school to junior high, saying she is intelligent enough but will not attend school regularly and shows no interest while she is there.

Now JoAnn is 14 and has discovered that she can make money from boys and men. She drops out of school, lives in one sparsely furnished room and does nothing. Nothing. She has no outfit that costs over twenty-five dollars; she attends political meetings which advertise free sandwiches and drinks.

Now she is in her twenties. She goes with a boyfriend to visit a male friend. One man is killed; the other goes to jail. JoAnn goes home—but she doesn't stay long. They say one of the friends kicked her. Anyway, she is in pain, loses weight, is in and out of the hospital.

"I got nothing to worry about," says JoAnn when the teacher visits her. "It don't cost me nothing."

On the day of her funeral, she comes into her own: there is a choir, the minister preaches a long sermon, there are flowers and telegrams. In death she is somebody.

Question: When did JoAnn die? At twenty-five, or at some earlier time?

"They" Are Manuel

To get to Manuel's house you have to squeeze down a narrow passageway that opens from an alley. The house is just two small rooms in a large, rambling, once beautiful home that is now rickety with age. The rooms are cold and bare. Manuel is sitting there. He has not gone to school again because he has no lunch and he has no shoes. That is why he is so frequently absent.

His family is large; his parents love him and are proud of his work in school. They are simply irrevocably poor. Manuel's IQ is 130+, and he has a particular aptitude in academic subjects and reads extremely well.

But he chooses vocational training. Although he wants more than anything to go on to high school and maybe become a professional man, he knows he cannot. He must get terminal education and go to work as soon as possible to help support the family.

His teacher arranges for him to get shoes, clothing, and free lunches. Together they work out a work-study schedule that includes a part-time job.

Manuel goes on field trips to Howard University, the vocational school, the Bureau of Engraving and Printing, the Library of Congress. He thinks about the educational opportunities in the armed services which will allow him to help his family with an allotment.

He decides to go on to high school and then join the armed services. He goes to a party. Some toughs crash the party and take offense because they are thrown out. They return. Manuel is shot through the head.

"They" Are Renée

Renée is a short, stocky, untidy girl with an unattractive gait. Her voice is low and harsh and she talks almost continually—often incoherently. Her classmates are all girls who have been kept back one or more grades and who are from poor families. She lives with her mother and two sisters in one room. Her father is gone; her mother and older sister are domestics.

Renée is subject to fits of rage and depression. She says no one loves her, that her mother and sister do not even like her. Her mother is at wit's end trying to manage Renée and is considering turning her over to the courts as "beyond parental control."

She is of average intelligence and enjoys sports, especially swimming. She works with crafts at her community center.

Because of Renée's emotional problems, she is sent to the counselor. But the counselor herself is neurotic and flies into rages with the students, frequently getting into fights with them. Renée is always worse after one of these sessions.

Her homeroom teacher tries to help Renée. She listens, and Renée talks—some truth, some fantasy, but much talk. During the talk sessions, Renée does not want the teacher to look at her. So the teacher listens while marking papers, writing on the board, or watering plants. Renée develops a crush on the teacher. She makes up excuses to stay in the homeroom. She makes presents constantly for the teacher. She likes to stay after school so she can walk the teacher home.

Though she is at odds with all the other teachers, Renée's attachment to her homeroom teacher grows. Still, she is disruptive in other classes and in the community center. She breaks all rules, teases and abuses smaller children, and is finally barred from the center for rowdy behavior.

Her homeroom teacher goes on maternity leave. Renée gets some clinical help and is later put in a foster home, where she transfers her crush to her foster mother. A year later she dies of tuberculosis.

"They" Are Wilfred

Wilfred's stepfather owns a cleaning and pressing shop. His real father lives somewhere else. His stepfather and mother are anxious for their son to conform, succeed, and do well. Wilfred has great aptitude for science and technology, but his parents insist that he take academic courses.

In school, Wilfred is considered slick, sly, and mischievous. His behavior alternates suddenly from a helpful, clean, courteous, and pleasant boy to one who is gloomy, morose, defensive; during these periods, he seldom studies, does careless work, and engages in mischief. His parents come to school frequently to discuss him.

The teacher writes to his parents to inform them of misconduct in school. They beat him severely and take away his privileges, as they always do when he misbehaves. Wilfred seems not to bear the teacher any ill will, but his behavior still varies from totally conforming to extremely destructive. When parental pressure becomes too great, he lies, becomes secretive and aggressive in school. The teacher and counselor try to convince his parents that Wilfred exhibits much good, constructive behavior and that they expect far too much from him.

In the spring, his parents propose to send him away to school. Wilfred is jubilant: he will be away from his parents. He is accepted in a military school where he wears a uniform, takes part in drills, and finds, at least partially, the accomplishment, security, prestige, and worthiness that he could not find at home or in school.

JoAnn, Manuel, Renée, Wilfred: those were some "different" students. They were strangers to me then—unlike my idea of students, unlike my own behavior as a student. They were alien—they were "they."

What I had to address myself to then, and what I have had to address myself to thereafter, was the nature of "they." Who are they? What are they like and why? And what does that make me? Clearly, they had to be identified before they could be understood. For only if I understood them could I be of any use to them as students and people and to myself as a teacher.

By "they" we mean students confined to city or country slums, cut off from the middle- or upper-class people who hear, speak, read, and write an English different from theirs. As teachers, we are often the only persons outside their group who have a chance to communicate with them. They may be immigrants to this country who speak another language, or native Americans from Puerto Rico, Hawaii, or Alaska who do not speak English. They may be American Indians for whom English is a second language. They may be students who speak one or more kinds of nonstandard English. Perhaps they speak one of the black dialects of South Carolina, Mississippi, or southern Illinois, or one of the white dialects in Appalachia. We may be teaching them in their home territories, or they may have come into the slums of the towns and cities bringing their language with them as immigrants do. They may be students whose mother tongue is a foreign language or dialect: Orientals or Europeans. Some are alienated white middle-class students, often from homes accustomed to producing conformist, suburban boys and girls who inevitably attend universities and become successful businessmen, lawyers, doctors, or other professionals. Some are black students, poor and middle class, discovering the genuine cultural heritage that has been denied to them. They may use standard English, nonstandard English, or both; they may be brilliant or average—but they are demanding to learn about black language and literature from teachers who know or are willing to learn about it. They are insisting that instructional materials be prepared for them and for other students who have not had the advantage of knowing the value of black culture.

They may be slow learners of several kinds. In some cases they simply learn at a slower rate than others do, and through the early years of school they have not been as mentally agile as others. These students are not mentally retarded or intellectually incompetent. Although they learn slowly, they often learn and retain more for longer periods. Unlike some of their more academically successful peers, they are not skimmers on the surface of learning—not facile, teacher-pleasing, verbal gymnasts. Frequently they are misunderstood by teachers who have not themselves been learners of this kind, and sometimes they are labeled "slow" by persons who do not understand their learning pattern. From this sometimes introspective group come inventors, physicists, and writers like Darwin, Edison, Faulkner, and Carver.

In other cases the slow learners are students who learn by using the eye as a secondary rather than primary data collector. They must listen or touch or use other senses for learning. These students do not always read well, but some listen extremely well. Others must move about and use their bodies actively to learn. They are made acutely uncomfortable when they are confined for hours, year after year, to seats in a classroom.

They may be students whose physical characteristics cause instant stereotyping. In the early years of school, boys must often be included in this group, because small boys are not always as neat as small girls and do not conform to school rules as easily. They do not write as legibly because their small-muscle development often comes later. Many women teach elementary school and assume that little girls who write neatly are smarter than messy little boys who do not. As a result, boys frequently think of themselves as less bright than girls and react accordingly. It is so unfortunate that some secondary school teachers read cumulative records which come in with the students and accept the evaluations they see, just as the students accept these evaluations of themselves.

Black students, too, especially those with pronounced Negroid features, are sometimes considered slower than others. Pseudoscientific theories about thick lips and tongues and about the redeeming virtues of white blood have been accepted, often subconsciously, by blacks and whites who should know better. Those maligned in this way include American Indians, Orientals, students who are poor and cannot dress well, students who are alienated and refuse to dress well, black students who wear the bush or the natural hairdo, white students with beards and long hair, deaf and partially sighted students, and all others who for any reason look different from our—the teachers'—idea of the typical American student. They are locked into the separateness we have created for them. They are "they." And as long as they are "they" to us, we will be "they" to them. In such prisons no learning and no teaching take place.

2

Learning about Language

A taxi passed and a man called out to the boy, "Man, why you ain't in school?" The boy smiled; the mother said softly, "He on'y four." Later, after asking his mother a question and getting an answer he liked, the boy laughed and jumped and said loudly, "Oh, we is!"

Not a single quoted sentence is standard, but I had no difficulty understanding either the language or the friendly interchanges among three people who understood and respected each other.

I wondered what would happen, though, when the little boy became five or six and started school. Would his teacher understand that his language, learned at home, had structure and form and consistency? Would his teacher accept him and his language, encouraging him to talk and then to read and write without constantly correcting him? Would his teacher wait until he was mature enough to choose for himself another language and then teach it without destroying his "home talk"?

In southern Maryland, recently, I was talking about language with a group of teachers and teacher aides. During the break a teacher came up to tell me about a consultant who had demonstrated "concept-building" with a group of youngsters. Because it was farm country and these were farm children, the consultant was building "concepts" about farms.

"What do you call the place where cows are kept?" she asked.

"A cowcuppin," the youngsters said.

She "corrected" them. "Oh, no, children. We call it a barn."

In their own rural territory this "concept-builder" was destroying, instead of learning from, the children's concepts.

As I worked with the teachers after the break, I asked how many had heard the word "cowcuppin." Smiles and nods showed that some had heard it. The word was completely new to me, so I wrote on the chalkboard:

COWCUPPIN

"Does it sound like this?" I asked. "Cowcuppin."

There were more nods, but one person suggested that I eliminate the "i" and use an apostrophe. I wrote:

COWCUPP'N

That was more like it, I judged from the murmurs of assent. I asked: "What is the home country of the people who live here?

"From what land might they have come?

"Where might a word like this have been used?"

A man at the back of the room suggested that the original word might have been "compound." Another suggested "cow pen." A third said "cows kept in." After a great deal of animated, interested talk, I admitted that I did not have any idea about the *real* derivation. I have talked with linguists since then about it, and only one has known the word.

Language is whatever stance a person takes and whatever sound he makes or transcribes that define him as a human being in his mind and in the minds of others. If a student stands, sits, walks, dresses, speaks, and writes in ways acceptable to the middle-class American, he has few problems in school. If he does not, he falls into the category of student with which this book is concerned.

The student reared in the inner city uses the language of his family and friends because that is what he hears, that is what he understands, and that is what he likes. The fact that he *likes* his own first language is important. Very important. We frequently overlook that fact when we begin language instruction. But it accounts for the consistent refusal of such students to "give up" their original language whatever we do, and for their reluctance to "learn" other modes of speech and written expression. Not only is language his identity, it is a source of joy, sensitivity, and power. With his language he can control many aspects of his environment and deal effectively with life as he knows it in his neighborhood. He can influence people, explain things he feels, tease, joke, and determine what is clever, right, stupid, and so on. He has, in short, all the personal affection normally found in any speaker's relationship to his own language style. As teachers trying to transmit the goals of education, we have too frequently damaged this affection by rooting out the nonstandard language and permitting few, if any, alternates. Immigrants, once they become "educated," return to their original language only sheepishly, or in situations of emergency, expediency, or humor. We all agree that it is not "practical" to speak anything other than standard English in the middle-class professions which we (rightly or wrongly) encourage our students to aspire to. Social approval and mobility, job security, professional advancement—all are bound up with "acceptable" language styles. But as teachers, we must commit ourselves to reducing the damage language attitudes have done and to developing the talents and facility of all speakers, *either in their first language or in another.*

The greatest damage is done by the assumption that language *reveals* levels of intellect. Our entire testing system is built on that erroneous assumption. Language tests reveal an ability to speak a language, not the ability to think. Without that clarification we are led into absurd conclusions: that all speakers with Oxford accents are intelligent; that children from the slums of Cleveland and Appalachia are intellectually deficient; that a poet is brighter than a mute sculptor—despite the fact that a nuclear physicist who spoke "good" English could not pass any language test devised by ghetto dwellers.

These assumptions are particularly specious when it comes to the poor. What we actually penalize is poverty. A French accent is charming, a Scotsman can write his folk idiom and wear a poet's crown for ages, a German's mispronunciation of "this" is logical. But when a black child says "I ain't got no mo'," that is somehow an outrage. This from people in a country notoriously reluctant to speak other languages abroad or learn them well at home. Every dialect seems somehow charming, except the dialect of the poor.

The complexity, the irony, the power, the sheer logic of black English, Puerto Rican English, and hill country English is not only missed, it is actively rejected. Yet consider, for example, the curious kind of verbal war called "capping," which takes place in black neighborhoods. In these sessions young men and boys develop their linguistic expertise in subduing an opponent. The ritual is never possible without an audience of peers who, like a chorus, egg the participants on and react to the successful "cap." Highly personal epithets and attacks are launched, but the end result is to strengthen each opponent's ability to receive and counter such challenges. When and if the session degenerates into a physical battle, the one who gets ruffled and strikes the first blow has "lost."

This ritual is known as *staggerlee,* and its elements are not only indicative of the love and feel for language these young people have, they are transferable into effective situations. One need only substitute other content and change the environment, and there emerges a debate in which students bring their talent and skills into play.

Language defines a person, and if we include stance, gestures, facial expressions, and sounds, then every human being has language—and uses it as his culture teaches him. All children *have* concepts, and it is our job to discover what the language is and what the concepts are. We should forget what we have heard about language deprivation and think of language differences.

In the Mississippi Delta, a four-year-old child said, "A catfish has a mouth like a big smile."
A nine-year-old boy in New York City said, "It's wings that makes birds fly. If I had me a pair of wings I'd fly out the window and people would look up at the sky and say, 'Why, there's Superman!' . . . And people saw me falling and they said, 'Why, that ain't Superman, that's a dead, dead, dead, long gone boy.' " [1]

---

[1] Paraphrased by Sandra Weiner in *It's Wings That Makes Birds Fly* (New York: Pantheon Books, 1968), p. 55.

Don't believe the researcher who says children do not have concepts, cannot think in abstract terms, are suffering from verbal deprivation. If, when they reach secondary school, they appear to be unable to listen, speak, read, and write well, do everything in your power to bring back to life that language power that has always existed in the student but may have been stunted by teachers who have relied on false assumptions about children.

Nonverbal Language

Students, like the rest of us, communicate in ways that do not involve speech.

A boy from the country, accustomed to working patiently with animals, might move slowly and quietly. Unaccustomed to meeting many new people, his eyes might never meet yours directly. A country girl might seem awkward and shy, looking at you out of the corners of her eyes. City students, on the other hand, may be aggressive or cocky. The boys often take a belligerent stance and assume the walk of new manhood—for black boys, it is a walk reportedly exactly like the walk some African boys assume immediately after traditional rites of puberty. The boys may wear hats in class, slouch in their seats, snatch items from the desks of others. The girls often attempt a sophisticated air—an assumption of womanhood, for they come from cultures which do not extend adolescence into the late twenties and thirties as in middle-class America.

Some teachers are offended by Spanish-speaking students who frequently stand close to them while speaking rapidly and directly. Others do not understand American Indians who stand far away, look down at the floor, and do not want to be touched by the teacher. Some ethnic groups gesture a great deal; others very little. Some students speak very little in the presence of adults and keep very still. Others are hyperactive and vocal. Some stare aggressively and seem to challenge the teacher to look away first. Attire, ways of walking, gestures, glances, mannerisms—all are aspects of nonverbal language and are influenced by family, culture, and peers.

Watch your classes for these evidences of nonverbal language, and remember that every group, all over the world, has its own. Indeed, you have yours, and your students will observe you as narrowly as you observe them to find signs of contempt, rejection, or weakness in your stance. Study their nonverbal language before criticizing or attempting to change it. If a change is tried too soon, the student feels that he and his culture are being rejected. And indeed they are.

Instead of attempting to make a permanent change in the verbal and nonverbal languages of culturally diverse students, the teacher should consider offering alternatives. No sensible person will deny that there is a dominant life style in this country—a fairly standard middle-class culture represented by most teachers and many businessmen. If a family, a community, a student, or group of students wishes to join that dominant group, there is every reason for the teacher to help, and many of the language arts techniques used in elementary school will be helpful. Second language techniques can be used for teaching English both to those who speak another language and those who speak a nonstandard dialect. Where there is no desire for a change, the teacher who insists is wasting his time. He should move into literature, reading, or some other aspect of English until there is an indication that a language change is wanted. Or, if the teacher is prepared, he can offer courses in language varieties, the American English language, dialect, or other courses like those recommended by linguists for preparing teachers. Secondary—even elementary—school is not too early for this.

Muriel Rukeyser, in her poem "Effort at Speech between Two People," speaks of a young girl who dreams of death and says that she would have jumped from a steep window if "the sun had not lighted clouds and plains." [2] That sun could well have been an understanding teacher.

Attitudes Toward Verbal Language

I *am* the language I speak and write, and an attack on my language is an attack on me. Many of the failures to improve speech, reading, and writing are the failures of teachers and specialists who have attacked and corrected the oral and written language of pupils as though it were an enemy to be vanquished. Textbooks have supported teachers in this kind of attack, and little attention has been paid in teacher-training or in textbook preparation to the really important other side of the issue. As Edwin Sauer asks, "What *is* good English?" He and Hans Guth, in their respective books, discuss this question in a way that will help you understand the language of your students and correct those who consider any dialect other than their own inferior, who speak of deprived and restricted language, usage errors, careless speech, and nonverbal students. [3] Do not join the teachers who brand students as disadvantaged, slow, and below average simply because the language they use is different. And do not fall into the trap of thinking that all facile users of standard English are intelligent. A young woman who teaches in a Chicago suburb spoke of the wealthy youngsters in their school who speak so well and are so

---

[2] Muriel Rukeyser, "Effort at Speech between Two People," in *A Treasury of Great Poems, English and American,* volume two, ed. and annotated by Louis Untermeyer (New York: Simon & Schuster, 1942; 1945), pp. 1219–1220. Reprinted by permission.

[3] See Chapters 1 and 3 of Edwin H. Sauer, *English in the Secondary School* (New York: Holt, Rinehart and Winston, 1961); see also Chapter 2 in Hans P. Guth, *English Today and Tomorrow* (Englewood Cliffs, N.J.: Prentice-Hall, 1964).

polite and verbal that it takes an astute teacher quite a while to find out how dull—sometimes retarded—some of them are.

Knowledge of what language is and how it develops is crucial, and acceptance of it—whatever its form—is important in the educational experience.

Whatever language or dialect is spoken in the home is the language or dialect spoken by a young child. This might be Spanish, an Indian tongue, standard American English (with regional variations), or nonstandard American English. The language of a rural area is not changed because a family moves to the city. The child's life outside the home begins early, and he adopts the language of his peers naturally. By the time children reach school they have already internalized one language and sometimes two or more of them.

For example, a Puerto Rican child in New York City might speak Spanish at home and a combination of nonstandard American English and Spanish among his peers. When he enters school and hears his teacher, he may learn for the first time that another language is spoken and preferred in the school. Everything then depends on the attitude of that teacher. The pedant who begins immediately to overcorrect can kill any desire to learn in this child; the patronizer can limit growth by expecting too little.

Given a chance to choose, any intelligent student will opt for his parents and his peers; given an initial complete acceptance, followed—when he is ready—with an explanation of what language is, and offered—again when he is ready—several alternatives, the student will not feel threatened or rejected but will more readily accept the feasibility of change and desirability of adding another language.

At all times the language resources of the pupil must be exploited. The teacher should learn what words and expressions pupils use, and should supply, with no value judgments, others that are standard American. Glossaries and dictionaries can be compiled in class to explore the wide variety of language uses and word definitions. If a class is so culturally diverse that many different words and phrases can be found, so much the better for students and teachers.

Language and geography can be correlated by language maps. Students can be encouraged to teach others words from their languages or dialects. In short, the first resource in language study must be the student himself. Language diversity is a strength, not a weakness.

What Can the Teacher Do about Language?

We must know more than what language is and what our attitude toward it should be. We must be armed with ways to teach students these things:

To accept and to understand their language and the language of others, nonverbal as well as verbal.

Some simple ideas about the geography and history of American English.

An understanding of how and why language changes.

The ability to use appropriate language and to shift, when necessary, among several different languages or levels of the same language.

Even without books or other instructional materials, some specific activities can establish the habit of oral exchange early in the teaching year. These are only recommendations; read them, and then devise ideas to suit your students.

Have the class count off by numbers, perhaps 1–2–3–4–5, and put all students with the same number together, thus providing for heterogeneous groupings. Give the following instructions to each group. All are to introduce themselves to each other and to plan ways for group introductions to the class. Suggest that perhaps some will want to tape information about themselves, some may simply introduce themselves individually, shy ones may ask a group leader to present them, or they may choose to discuss common interests in a panel. While the planning goes on, visit each group and listen. If you have a small cassette tape recorder you may record some groups or individuals unobtrusively. In this version of D.T.A., you are in the background observing nonverbal and verbal language, learning how your students work and talk together. Begin a folder for each student at this point and keep it consistently as long as you teach the student.

A second suggestion is that you prepare and pass out—or have students prepare, then shuffle and exchange—instructions for a brief verbal activity. You need not know what particular instruction each has received. Illustrate first the kinds of verbal activities you expect, such as:

Stand and tell your full name and two other facts about yourself.
Come to me or go to a classmate and recite your favorite foods.
Describe today's weather (temperature, precipitation, and so on).
(These instructions can be played on a tape recorder, and students in turn can follow instructions.)

A third suggestion is that you play such familiar games as Twenty Questions, or ask students to describe and illustrate games they enjoyed playing as young children. You may find that interesting arguments ensue as students learn that familiar games have different rules and words in various parts of this country or that there are variations played in other lands.

Give brief, well-known phrases or words that have different meanings in various places:

the flood (the Bible story, mythology, reality in some places)
spider (arachnids, a skillet, a "corner" of liquor)
Lorna Doone (a story, a cookie, a biscuit in England)

These suggestions are designed to establish the varieties of language and culture present in the class. For whatever culturally distinct group we teach, we must use the customs, elements, and competences of that group to develop the intellect and skills of the user. I am not suggesting a major anthropological survey to motivate these young people, but the simple, accessible, common-sense means by which the connection between language and life can be made. An examination of the source literature of a group should present innumerable possibilities for language instruction and motivational activities. By source literature, I mean the myths and folklore—the dream literature of a people. In this dream literature lies the key to their values, mores, and archetypes. Deep in the Br'er Rabbit stories, when uncorrupted and retold in their original form, is the wise hare of Africa. The transmission of this folk story character to the New World is most interesting. Annacy, the spider deity of West Africa who is a divine trickster and shaman, becomes an outlaw in the New World, secretive, elusive, cunning, deceptive, with all the characteristics of the cunning Odysseus without his power. Annacy takes the form of a rabbit or monkey (always the weakest of the animals) who uses wit to protect himself from the burdens and oppressions of a slave society and later an oppressive society. It is from this folk character that the staggerlee tradition comes, the triumph of a weaker over a stronger as a result of cunning, verbal skill, and wit—the cockiness and braggadocio that the smaller animal uses as a cover for his physical vulnerability. These are examples of archetypes carried into the day-to-day life of a people in their expressions, their values, and their style.

The following is a typical folk story.

Whip Me
Why Riley Rabbit Doesn't Have to Work [4]
Margaret Taylor Burroughs

Once there was a great disturbance in Riley Rabbit's neighborhood. A big bossy lion named Leonard moved in and made life miserable for all of the animals. Leonard Lion destroyed so many pigs and goats until it looked like, if things kept up this way, the whole neighborhood and everything in it would be ruined.

Riley called all the animals together for a meeting to see what could be done. After arguments this way and that way and back and forth they decided to send Leonard Lion word that they would feed him, but he would have to stay in the house and behave himself, and if he didn't do that, they would put the law on him and throw him in the calaboose.

"Well, gentlemen," said Fred Fox, "now that we have decided what to do about this problem, who will carry the word to Leonard Lion?"

"I wouldn't mind doing it," said Bobby Bear, "but I'm way behind in my corn planting, and I just don't have the time."

---

[4] Margaret Taylor Burroughs, Director, DuSable Museum in Chicago, "Why Riley Rabbit Doesn't Have to Work," from *Whip Me Whop Me Pudding.* Reprinted by permission.

"I would go myself," said Fred Fox, "but my stock are all perishing for water, and I have to go and dig a well."

"I can't go," spoke up Gussie Goose. "I've got to cut the grass in my yard." Everyone looked at Tom Turkey Gobbler. "Don't look at me," he said. "My wife is sick with a misery in her back, and I've got to go home and tend the children."

"I have to go and root up my garden before it rains," spoke up Perry Pig quickly.

Riley Rabbit listened patiently to all of their excuses.

"By golly, folks!" he said. "If you are all afraid of Leonard Lion, I'm not. I'm going to go down there and tell that old lion just what we're going to do for him and what we are not. And if he doesn't like it he can lump it. Just wait here for me and I'll show you."

With that, Riley tucked his britches legs down in his boots, pulled his cap to the side of his head, stuck his cigar in his mouth, and sauntered down the road to Leonard Lion's house just as if he was going to a picnic.

Now Riley walked biggity as long as the animals were watching him, but when he got round the bend in the road, he put the cigar out, straightened the cap on his head and began to walk mighty different. When he got to Leonard's house, he crept up to the door and knocked on it. "Mr. Lion," he whispered weakly, "are you there?"

Leonard Lion came to the door. "Who are you and what do you want?" he roared.

"It's me, Riley Rabbit," said Riley in a weak voice. "Mr. Lion, the animals had a meeting and they sent me here to tell you—to explain to you—that they had decided since you were such an important person tht it wasn't right for you to have to go out and get your own vittles. They told me to tell you that if you will stay in your house all the time instead of going out foraging for food, that they will send food down here to you."

"I've got to have fresh meat every day three times a day," roared Leonard Lion. "If I can have it, I'll stay in my house but if I can't I'll come out and destroy everything and everybody in this town."

"Yes sir, Mr. Lion," said Riley. "They'll do that. They'll feed you good, too. I'll see to that myself!" With that Riley took off down the road lickety split. As soon as he was out of Leonard Lion's sight he stopped and knocked the dust off of his boots. He pulled his cap back over on the side of his head, stuck the cigar back in the side of his mouth, and strutted back to where the animals were waiting for him.

They all ran to meet him. "Did you see him, Riley?" they asked. "Did you see Leonard Lion? What did he say?"

"Did I see him?" said Riley Rabbit, biggity-like. "I went down there to see him, didn't I? Of course I saw him!"

"What did you tell him? Weren't you afraid?"

Riley snatched his cap from his head and threw it down on the ground and stomped on it. "Afraid! What foolishness are you talking about now?" Riley doubled up his fist and shook it in their faces. "Why, I'm a man! A M–A–N! And I'm not afraid of nothing or nobody and that means Leonard Lion and all the rest!"

Then the animals begged Riley to tell them about it.

"Well," said Riley, "I went down to Leonard's house and banged on the door. When he opened it I went in and sat down by the fire. I told Leonard that we had decided that he was raising too much disturbance in the neighborhood. I told him that he had better stay in his house and behave or else we would beat his liver out. Then I told him that he would have to take what we gave him to eat and like it, or else he could lump it!"

"Gee, Riley," exclaimed the animals. "You sure are brave!"

"That's because I'm a man," said Riley. "A M–A–N! Why, Leonard Lion pitched and roared but that didn't scare me none. When he saw that I meant business, he said he would do just what we told him. So that's how it was!"

Then the animals tried to decide who would be the first to feed Leonard Lion. Everyone said to the other, "You go first! You go first!" They argued and quarreled among themselves until Riley said, "Let's draw straws and the one who pulls the shortest one will feed Leonard Lion first." They held the straws and they all pulled. Gussie Goose drew the shortest one. Gussie began to shiver and shake.

"Oh, no!" she whined.

"Go on, Gussie," said Riley. "Go on and feed Leonard Lion like you agreed to do." So Gussie Goose went down and Leonard Lion ate her up.

The next feeding time Perry Pig drew the short straw. "Wait! "Wait!" he cried.

"Wait, my eye!" said Riley Rabbit. "Do on down there and feed Leonard Lion or else we'll drag you down there!" So Perry Pig went down, and Leonard Lion ate him up, too.

Now Fred Fox and Alec Alligator soon saw that as long as Riley held the straws, he would send everyone down to be eaten except himself. At the next feeding time they fixed it so that Fred Fox held the straws, and, sure enough, Riley drew the short one.

When Riley saw that, he said to himself, "I sure got my business twisted that time." But out loud he said, "Folks, it looks as if my time has come. We've all had a lot of fun together but all that is behind me now. I have to go and feed Leonard Lion. I've tried to be a good neighbor to all of you and now that my time has come, I want all of you to pray for me and promise me that when your time comes you'll meet me in the promised land. Well, goodbye, folks." And with that he started walking down the road.

Riley sounded so pitiful that all of the animals started crying. Riley walked along slowly as if he was indeed going to his funeral. He decided that even if Leonard Lion did have to wait for his dinner that he would take one last look around the old neighborhood. He went to his house and the barn and the hog lot. Then he went down to the well for one last drink of water. He looked down in it and saw his own sad face shining up from the bottom.

Then Riley suddenly got an idea. He rushed off pell-mell for Leonard Lion's house. When he got there he knocked on the door and said, "Mr. Lion, here is your dinner."

Leonard Lion threw open the door. "It's a mighty little dinner you brought and it's mighty late at that!" Leonard looked at his watch and showed his sharp teeth. Riley's knees shook worse than ever.

"Yes sir, Mr. Lion," he said. "I'm sorry but I just couldn't get here any sooner. If I'm not enough for your dinner I know where there is a lot of good fresh meat that I saved for you. I'll show it to you if you will come with me."

"Where is this meat?" asked Leonard.

"It isn't far," said Riley. "I put it up for you right near my house."

"It had better be enough," said Leonard, and they set out for Riley's house. Riley led him up to the well. He opened it and looked in and then jumped back.

"Goodness! Mr. Lion," said Riley. "He's in there eating up all your meat right now."

When Riley said that, Leonard pushed him away from the well and looked

down himself. He thought he saw another lion down there looking up at him.
"Who are you?" roared Leonard Lion.
"Who are you?" Leonard's voice echoed back up the well.
"You heard him, didn't you, Mr. Lion?" said Riley. "He's mocking you. Are you going to let him get away with it? And stealing your meat at the same time, too! If he would come up here I'd whip him myself."
Leonard Lion looked down the well and roared, "Who-oo-oo-oo?"
The voice came back, "Who-oo-oo-oo?"
"Stand back, Riley Rabbit!" said Leonard, and he made a dash and jumped into the well. As soon as Riley heared Leonard hit the water he slammed the cover shut and locked it. Then he pulled his cap over to the side of his head, put his cigar in his mouth, and sauntered down the road to where the animals were debating who was to feed Leonard Lion next. When they saw Riley they thought he was a ghost.
"Riley," they asked, "didn't Leonard eat you up?"
"Eat me up?" said Riley in disdain. "I wasn't aiming to be eaten up by that old lion or anyone else."
"What did he say? What did he say? Is he coming up here to destroy us all?"
"Look, folks," said Riley Rabbit, "you don't have to be afraid of anything or anyone as long as you have a man like me around. When that old lion tried to get me I beat him half to death and threw him in the well near my house and drowned him. If you don't believe me, go down there and see for yourself."
The animals went and looked into the well and sure enough, there was Leonard Lion drowned at the bottom of the well.
"You're a brave and smart man, Riley," said all of the animals. "From this time on, you won't have to work no crop because we will do it for you." And that's why Riley lives off other folk.

Get your students involved in explaining the values and personalities of the characters. Where do their sympathies lie? Do they want the rabbit to win? Why? Is this like watching a clever jewel thief and wishing he could get away? Or is there something else in the basic nature of the rabbit that evokes sympathy? Is it his smallness? His cleverness? His honesty with himself when alone? Or does the character call up hostile emotions? Who, in the class, is on the side of the bigger animals? What about the goose? What is the reaction to this truly innocent victim? These questions should stir a good deal of class discussion and lead effortlessly into writing assignments. For a special kind of innovation, use this story as a transition into the folk myths of other lands. Particularly good for this story is Homer and the story of Ulysses and the Cyclops. What is Ulysses' objection to the land of the Cyclopes? (They were not civilized, did not till the land or organize themselves into efficient groups.) In relation to the Cyclopes, Ulysses is like the rabbit—small and helpless. Like the rabbit, he must use his wits. How does he do this? When, if ever, do we feel pity for the one-eyed giant? Read aloud the Cyclops' conversation with the ram as he leaves the cave. Relate the taunting of Ulysses as he rows away in the boat with the rabbit's taunting. How is the goose like the crew, eaten by the Cyclopes? These and other questions ought to make a good transition into the reading of Homer, but a reading more sound, more interesting, more useful because it began with the study of something the student knew about, reacted to, and could bring with him into the reading of another kind of literature.

It is in just such ways as these, and there are many other possibilities, that we should be directing our energy when beginning language instruction for these students. Similar kinds of lessons are being done by members of our profession everywhere, with other culturally distinct groups. A comparison with the folklore of Spanish, Indian, and other groups is inevitable and recommended.

3

Arts and Skills of Language

Language is not simply a skill; it is first and foremost an art. A baby comprehends language long before he acquires its skills. He squirms and cries for food and attention. Later he plays with the sounds of language in his babbling stage. He listens, responds to what he hears, then imitates. He waves his arms and legs in joy or anger. At this stage there is little skill but a great deal of art in his nonverbal and verbal communication.

Some studies are beginning to suggest that all humans are born with the capability for language, an ability that distinguishes them from animals. Talking birds and animals simply imitate; people do not. Some apes can be taught sign language but not speech. All babies who can see and hear and who have intellect are capable of learning language. And they do learn it, long before they enter school. African and Swiss youngsters learn three or more at one time.

Skill in language develops when the child sees that he is not communicating effectively and tries to improve his speech to get something he wants. Along with this effort to make himself clearly understood is a fascination with language for the fun of it—and the fun of language lies in its art. We have all heard children who think they are unobserved repeating sentences and words over and over again, practicing the same sounds, different sounds, rhymes. They imitate people and things they have heard. They invent words.

Although listening, speaking, reading, and writing are almost inextricably interwoven as "language arts" or "communication arts and skills," they are treated separately here except when an example from one of the arts clarifies another. And it is important to keep in mind that the intangible but extremely important art of reasoning or thinking must be considered part of all four aspects.

Listening

Listening is first among the language arts because through it the young child learns and imitates the sounds of language. However accurate his learning and imitation of the language he has heard, he may nevertheless have great difficulty, for any number of reasons, when he enters secondary school.

If he is from a noisy or threatening environment, he may have "tuned out" so that he does not listen.

If his home has been the quiet country or a home where silence is valued, he may tune out because the school is too noisy and threatening.

If he is accustomed to failure, in school or out, and is shouted at by parents or teachers, he may refuse to listen or respond because he dreads failing again.

If he is alienated from society in general, he may choose to turn himself off in school, listening to nothing, or to inner voices.

If he is deaf or partly deaf, or if he suffers from hunger or any physical defect, he may be unable to listen.

If he does not see himself as a real or worthy person, he may conclude that he is unable to learn.

We, as secondary school teachers of English, have the responsibility of determining the listening abilities of our students. Physical or emotional disorders, of course, should be referred to the school nurse, guidance counselor, psychologist, or to someone in the school who diagnoses and treats such difficulties. Some schools, however, simply do not provide these services. Unfortunately, these are often the schools made up of students who are poor and who come from diverse cultures that need these services most. If that is the circumstance, then it is up to us to work with students who have listening problems. These are some ways to find out who they are.

Read aloud or tape instructions and ask the class to follow them exactly. Let the class know that this is not a test, that you will repeat if a hand is raised to request this. Read, or play the tape, softly the first time. Note and record those who request a repeat.

Try the same kind of exercise daily for at least a full week, taking only a small part—perhaps ten minutes—of class time.

If you make some of the instructions unusual or funny, you may engage the interest of those who are tuned out or tuned off. Watch faces during each exercise for signs of straining to hear.

One sample of instructions might be:

Write your name, last name first, on the top line of your paper.
On the second line, print your name, first name first.
Put your middle initial on the third line. If you have no middle initial, write an X on that line.
If you have a telephone, write the number on the fourth line.
If you have a dog, write "dog" in a square on line 5.
If you have a cat, write "cat" in a circle on line 5.
If you have another pet, put a circle in a square on line 5.

This can go on, can be shorter, and can become quite complicated as the class becomes accustomed to the drill. Since success is what you want, repeat the instructions from the end to the beginning to let students check and see how well they did.

Sometimes your instructions can involve moving objects around or even having students move. For example:

> If you have a yellow pencil, hold it up.
> Put your pen on the ledge of the desk on your right.
> Place a book on the desk to your left.
> All boys stand.
> All girls hold up their right hand.

You can devise listening games using pencils, earrings, buttons, or books just to gain listening interest, determine problem areas, and improve ability to listen carefully. And let students help by making up other games. If there are several students who speak another language, select a bilingual student to translate your instructions; otherwise a teacher or a friend can help you tape instructions in another tongue.

The tape recorder can be used effectively to coordinate listening skills with other language arts. For example, a tape can be made of recognizable sounds arranged in a plot sequence. After listening to the sounds, students can describe in writing what they think took place. The first of these sound sequences should be short and uncomplicated; later they can be longer and may even be based on a story or film the class knows. This is a typical wordless sound sequence.

1. Alarm clock
2. Feet moving on floor
3. Running water
4. Feet going down steps
5. Dishes and breakfast sounds
6. Door slams
7. Car starts, fails to catch, starts
8. Car moves rapidly
9. Train sound approaches
10. Crash

(This exercise, and others like it, was developed by the Great Cities Language Arts Program in Washington, D.C., directed by Louis Kornhauser.)

Sequences can be based on Aesop's fables, narrative poems, short stories, and short films. Or students can produce their own sequences.

Other listening arts and skills can be allied with speaking, reading, and writing—even with literature and the humanities. Later chapters discuss listening to recorded music and literature.

Speaking

The importance of accepting and encouraging speech—not interfering with it unless the student understands he needs help and requests it—cannot be overemphasized. We must devise more ways to encourage students to speak. Creating an atmosphere of trust and relaxation is important in getting students to ask questions of the teacher and one another. Simple freedom to question is a good way to get students talking.

In our secondary school and college days, we become accustomed to the lecture method, with an all-knowing instructor giving us the word of truth. We must forget that method now. Our students have already had teachers who have practically talked them out of school—certainly out of any desire to listen. Now is our chance to involve them; to open them to learning; to give them a chance to find out what their resources are, and to use these resources to become better talkers, thinkers, learners.

We must learn to ask the kinds of questions which will make students think seriously about what they want to know. Why are you here? What is important to learn? What do you need to know to survive in the world?

Neil Postman and Charles Weingartner, in *Teaching as a Subversive Activity,* say:

> Generally speaking, these [disadvantaged] children are reputed to be "slower" learners than other types of children. If this is true, it simply means that they do not function so well as others *in the existing school environment.* It cannot be inferred from this that "disadvantaged children" would be a "problem" if the ecology of the school environment were entirely different.[1]

Some of the questions these authors suggest students be asked are: What bothers you most about adults? Why? What, if anything, seems to you to be worth dying for? How can you tell "good guys" from "bad guys"? What other "language" does man have besides that of words?

Another suggestion to get students asking and answering questions is to tell the class that a black attaché case contains a computer which could answer any question. Students asked and then decided to ask only those questions to which answers were not already known. They listed questions to ask about the questions and decided that a question list helped a person to know what he is talking about, what kind of information he wants, whether a question can be answered, and what must be done to find an answer.

Giving students a speaking voice through questions is an extremely sound and effective means to encourage speech. In any textbook, old or new, there are some pretty bad suggestions about speaking. In examining these sugges-

---

[1] Neil Postman and Charles Weingartner, *Teaching as a Subversive Activity* (New York: Delacorte Press, 1969), p. 80.

tions, we should not confuse etiquette and getting students ready for the job world with getting them to think. Certainly, they can learn to use the telephone, give oral reports, or role-play applying for jobs. They can even learn how to introduce people to each other. But first they must speak about what is important to them, and we must listen and encourage them to question us, each other, and the society in which they live. If the art of questioning comes first, skill in speaking will follow.

Children usually learn to write long after they listen and speak; some do not write at all before they come to school. But writing is not just language put down in visual symbols. English, in fact, does not really lend itself to that kind of representation. Writing as an art is mastered by very few; writing as a skill is difficult for most students but especially for those outside middle-class America.

Students who are "different" often come to secondary school unwilling to write. For the same reasons that they have turned off listening and refused to speak, they avoid written expression. Those who do not speak English do not write it either; those who use nonstandard English find it pointless to seek a sound-for-symbol correspondence. Ken Goodman, in a reference to this, speaks of the child who asked the teacher to spell "rat." When the teacher said "r–a–t," the child impatiently replied, "I don't mean 'rat-mouse'; I mean 'rat *now.*'"[2]

Feeling comes first. For too many years the emphasis in this country has been on expository writing in secondary school.[3]

Ways to Elicit Writing

The simple techniques described in Margaret Landon's book, *Let the Children Write*,[4] are graphic. I used this book, modifying the techniques to suit my students, when I was teaching in England.

I passed every student a sheet of paper and explained that I wanted a written word or phrase on each line as I gave the cue.

1. There's a spider on the wall. Jot down a word or a phrase telling how you feel.
2. Briefly describe his legs.

---

[2] Ken Goodman, "Dialect Barriers to Reading, "*Elementary English,* Vol. 42 (December 1965), pp. 853–860.

[3] In England, on the other hand, recent emphasis has been in quite the opposite direction—that is, toward narrative, descriptive prose. For a clear look at what such writing can be like, see the examples of student writing in *Growth through English,* a report based on the Dartmouth Seminar, 1966.

[4] Margaret Landon's *Let the Children Write* (London: Longmans, 1961) is an explanation of intensive writing.

3. Now tell something about his body.
4. Describe a spider web early in the morning.
5. Tell how the spider feels as he waits in his web.
6. Now, write a final feeling about the spider that has caught a bug.
7. How do you feel now?

I gave every student a chance to write, then collected papers. Some used single words, some only phrases, some sentences, some a combination. Here is an example:

1. Ugh!
2. Legs are hairy, ugly, sticky.
3. His body is round and bloated.
4. The web is silver with dew.
5. He crouches waiting to pounce.
6. He feels happy.
7. Ugh!

Another way to structure writing to help students know for sure that they can write—and that is the initial purpose—is to ask a series of questions for which answers must be words or short phrases. For example:

What is one of the most beautiful things you have ever seen?
How did it make you feel?
What is the ugliest thing you have seen?
How did you feel then?
What would you think if you saw these things together?
Can you write one word describing the beautiful object?
One word describing the other?

Here is a sample student paper:

My mother's smile
Warm
The frown of my enemy
Frightened and tense
Unhappy and ready to run
Lovely
Cruel

Of course, questions can be much more sophisticated than these and may grow from stories heard or read, questions raised in class, or from the student's efforts to learn more about language.

The written language of a student is much like his oral language, and we must be careful to avoid overcorrection of either if we are to encourage the student to write. Some other specific ways to encourage a student follow.

Keep a folder for every student, and file the folders by class and name so they are readily accessible to you and to the students as well as to tutors or lay readers and parents. If possible, avoid marking or grading these papers. Instead, write encouraging comments about the good things you see, and use some color other than red for this. You may wonder what difference a color makes, but when students have for years associated red with corrections and continuing failures on their papers, it does make a difference when they see words of praise written in blue or green.

Ask every student to keep a journal, and assure each student that, although you want him to write in it every day, you will read it only when invited, and even then you will not grade it. You will have to think of stimulating ways to encourage daily personal writing for students who have never done this before. You might write your own journal the summer before you begin teaching and share it with your students. Read to them your personal reflections about what you see and hear, comments about books and plays, happy or sorrowful happenings in your life, disappointments and joyful occasions, such as a wedding or a funeral you have attended. This is a way of showing yourself as a human being to your students as well as encouraging them to write.

Read parts of other journals to your classes. They may enjoy some of Lady Bird Johnson's daily recollections about her life in the White House or Theodore Roosevelt's earlier ones. If you know a policeman, ask him to let you use his daily memo pad (they are public property).

Using models for writing is a fruitful experience for these students, because you can select works written by people from their own cultures. They will recognize the language of their people and share that recognition with students from other cultures. If you do this, however, be sure to do it regularly, and include a piece of work representing each ethnic group in your class. The initial piece should be brief, and students may have to be helped to recognize and imitate the language used. For example, if you have students from Appalachia in your class, you might use this selection from Jesse Stuart's *God's Oddling:*

"Land hogs air pizin as copperhead snakes," Uncle Mel said, then he fondled his long white beard in his hand. Uncle Mel was eighty-two years old, but his eyes were keen as sharp pointed briars and his shoulders were broad and his hands were big and rough. He had been a timber-cutter all his days and he was still a-cuttin' timber in West Virginia at the age of eighty-two. "He can't do this to ye, Mick!" [5]

You can reproduce this excerpt entirely, or you can write it sentence by sentence on the board. Students who are familiar with country or mountain

---

[5] Jesse Stuart, *God's Oddling* (New York: McGraw-Hill Book Co., 1960), p. 61.

dialect can be resources for understanding the vocabulary. You might ask questions like these:

> Can you say the first sentence the way I would say it?
> What is a copperhead snake?
> What do you think a land hog is?
> Can you describe a briar?
> What does a timber cutter do?

When the students understand the selection, ask them to use it as a model and to write about a person they know, using the same sentence order. Something like this might come from an inner-city student:

> "Landlords is filthy as gray rats," Aunt Martha said, and placed her wrinkled brown arms on her hips. Aunt Martha was sixty-three years old, and her eyes were weak as a newborn baby's and her shoulders were stooped and her hands were red and rough. She had been a day worker all her life and she was still a-doing day's work in Long Island at the age of sixty-three. "He can't do this to us, John."

The effort of thinking through what someone else has said, and the additional one of writing a comparable piece of work, is both rewarding and stimulating. The student who says he is unable to think of a subject has that problem solved; the student who needs practice gets it; the student who needs recognition as a member of a different group receives it. If, after writing from a model, the students want to read the book it is from, be sure it is available.

Before leaving the subject of using models for writing, I should say that it is perfectly possible to have a different model for each student after working through group writing exercises. Marking certain sections of paperback books—a different one for each student—and asking each to write is one way. You will have difficulty keeping them from reading the books, so don't try. Let them go on reading when they have finished writing; then perhaps they will write journal entries about the books, and you will have hooked them on both reading and writing.

Although writing should be shared since it is intended for an audience, we must be especially careful with these students, always accentuating the positive. For example, read compositions that are especially good aloud to the class. Name the writer if you know students will like this; otherwise do not.

Prepare a transparency of a very good paper and share it with the class, letting students point out with you the things that are good about it. Again, your naming the writer depends on your knowledge of your students.

Mimeograph or ditto and pass out several compositions without naming the writers. Ask students to write comments about the papers, comparing them for thought, content, and style. Do not consider or permit students to pick at the mechanics here *unless* that is the purpose of the lesson.

Display papers on the bulletin board. Allow students to arrange these displays and make an effort, within the year, to include a paper from each student. Writing from models lends itself to such displays, for the original can be placed in the center with the student writings surrounding it. Compositions about pictures can be displayed in the same way.

How can you go about correcting student writing if you are to avoid red penciling?

Select the kind of error made by many students and *you* write a composition illustrating this error more than once. Then either write your composition on the board, prepare a transparency for the overhead projector, use the opaque projector for your paper, or make multiple copies for the class. Ask the class to mark your composition, leading them by careful questioning to see what they are looking for. Ask them to look at their writing to see whether they have done this kind of thing. You may then prepare or select another model with the kind of writing that gives practice in avoiding the error. In this way no one student is attacked, no papers are bloody, and students have found for themselves ways to improve writing.

Another way to encourage personal writing is to ask students to write letters to you about what interests them. This is a way of correlating the art of writing with the discussion. The letters can go deeply into the questions students are concerned about. Instead of marking or grading the letters, write answers to them. Your answers may take time, but it also takes time to attack and mark letters. Your letters will be in correct form and will be personal. Here those attitudes listed in Chapter 1 are crucial. Your attitude is accepting if you keep the letters in confidence, accept them without correcting, and are honest and open in your answers. You will have involved yourself in what you want students to do well, and you will be providing a model for them.

All notes, business letters, and memoranda should be read in this way. There must be a purpose for them, and they should be mailed, with answers expected. School for these students has too often been an unreal experience, separated from the lives they lead. We can help make it real for them through their writing.

Reading

Reading, like listening, is a receptive art and skill, while speaking and writing demand an audience. It is more than the ability to sound out written symbols for spoken words, more than the ability to say those words, phrases, and sentences aloud or silently. It is more than understanding what each word means, more than an ability to answer questions about the material. These things are all parts of reading, and they can be taught in school. But reading is more than this.

Reading is receiving many kinds of messages from whatever is written —understanding and enjoying the messages. It is becoming a part of what is read and feeling with the author what the author intends the reader to feel. It is the art of accepting a communication from an unseen person who may have lived hundreds of years ago and lives today only in the words he wrote. It is the art of moving into that world and exploring the words for a deeper knowledge of the writer and his intention. It is the art of accepting a communication from a person in another place and going with him to that place. It is the art of seeing and recognizing (or learning for the first time) the contemporary world and knowing how to separate the real from the unreal, the true from the false. This is the art of reading. And the best of it is a private experience which will bear no interference.

Skill in reading does include knowing the sounds of letters and recognizing combinations of letters—being able to say and to understand words, phrases, clauses, paragraphs. But it is also knowing how to get meaning from a poem, an essay, a short story, or a problem in mathematics. It is recognizing many words at once and getting some understanding of several sentences through a quick glance at key words.

Students from culturally diverse backgrounds are not always good readers. Some, whose families have given them a sense of pride in and respect for themselves and their culture, are. Black, brown, red, or yellow—if they have heard stories, rhymes, poems, and folktales at home, they have heard the rhythm of the language they will read. And they usually read well, if the reading they do is in that language, but they will not necessarily read English well. However, if they have been encouraged to think of themselves as persons able to learn new things, they will try and will often be successful.

We have all read a lot about why black children cannot read. Color has nothing to do with it. Black children who have heard stories and who have books in their homes—books they see being read and are shared with them— have no difficulty as long as their teachers expect them to learn.

Other minorities in our diverse population have a harder time—those with few or no books in their homes, who have heard talk and tales in another language, or who see themselves as different even before they enter school. That the responsibility for their trouble lies with us and our system can be made clear by considering the kind of students and teaching in the United Nations school in New York. There the children come from everywhere, but they are primarily upper- and middle-class children. So the black African child, the Oriental, or the East Indian is not subject to expectations of failure— his environment is, in aspiration and manner, more like that of middle- and upper-class Americans. Color and cultural diversity is not only not a handicap, it is an asset, used for the enrichment of all. Take that same child from the UN school, put him in a slum school, and he will soon be given the kind of careless instruction and formidable guidance that other slum or rural children are accustomed to.

Those of us who are teaching in secondary schools should know how elementary schools affect later reading ability and interest. Children are placed in reading groups, and they always know just as well as the teacher does whether they are in the fast, average, or slow group. Euphemisms like blue-birds, redbirds, and blackbirds are used, but the children always know.

For years terrible readers with controlled vocabularies have been used in elementary reading programs. They are boring and repetitious, with little literary value. The good readers get through them quickly, but even they lose some of their joy in reading. The others are struck with them, struggling with words which hardly make sense and are not interesting even when they do. The language actually used by children is not seen in these books. Who has ever heard a sensible six-year-old say, "Look! Look! Look!"? Luckier young-sters are taught with language approaches in which the teacher uses the words of children to write their own stories.

Secondary school students bring to you many problems grounded in their earlier teachers' failure to understand and to use the resources of the children. Here are some of those failures which must be recognized and avoided:

Not using the language of children as a rich resource.   "Cowcuppin" was mentioned as a word a student knew was used for a place in which cows are kept. Do you know the many meanings of *tough, dig,* or *bread?*

Depending too much on standardized tests to determine reading ability.   Peo-ple who speak a different language or dialect have different vocabularies and work at different speeds. If they are also poor, they may be hungry or sleepy, have failed to do well on tests in the past, or have low expectations which they repeatedly confirm. And when those who give the tests talk in a different way, do not seem to expect success, and show it, the student will sometimes not even make an effort. I have seen many students simply make interestintg designs on the answer sheet without ever looking at the questions.

Using the same approaches in secondary school which have already failed when used in elementary school.   The same books are sometimes used; this is insult-ing to the student who has had the book before—whose younger brothers and sisters may be using it now.

Accepting the "one right way" thesis.   Some school systems adhere to one method of teaching reading and insist that all teachers use it. This is folly. Students have different learning styles; teachers instruct in different ways. If we are going to teach a diverse student population, we must know and use many different methods to teach reading. And we must never stop learning new ways, modifying old ways, inventing ways to suit our learners.

Modified Language Experience

Try using the questions from the Speaking section of this chapter to suggest that students do a group story about what they consider worth dying for, for example. Write, or let a student leader write, the experience on the board as it develops. This may well turn out to be a poem, a story, or an essay. Make copies of the "language experience" and permit students to read it to you or to each other. Let them make changes. Within a term you should have a collection of such group experience readings. This can form a book to be illustrated by students; or, if each student has a copy, each one may illustrate his own book.

Any of the compositions prepared as suggested in the section on writing can be used. The models are especially useful since both the original, taken from literature, and the copy can be read. Here, students may want to read their own efforts.

Some of the second-language techniques, to be discussed in Chapter 4, can be used, especially when you want to help students with the stress, pitch, and intonation of standard American English.

Modified Fernald Method

Grace Fernald discovered that among many learning styles, the kinesthetic had been neglected.[6] Boys in particular often seem to learn through their fingers rather than their eyes. After teaching a number of disadvantaged youngsters, I learned this method at UCLA. Then I modified it to suit my circumstances; I suggest that you modify mine to suit yours.

This method works best with a small group, but the group may be working within a larger class which is using different methods. You will need:

> A typewriter.
> A large file box for each student, with flash cards to fit.
> A notebook for each student.

Each student writes a short story or statement about anything that interests him. (Again, you may use the kinds of questions suggested in the Speaking section of this chapter.)

While he is writing, the student may ask you to supply any words he does not know. Write each word in large script on the flash cards. When he has finished, have him read the story to you, and write any words he has misspelled on separate flash cards for him. Help him with any word he cannot say.

Then have him trace each word he has asked for with his finger, pronouncing the syllables as he traces. When he thinks he knows the word, he can turn the flash card over and write it. If he forgets, he can trace again.

---

[6] Grace Maxwell Fernald, *Remedial Techniques in Basic School Subjects* (New York: McGraw-Hill Book Co., 1943).

The flash cards are filed in each student's box in alphabetical order, and he can always refer to the words for future stories, retrace them, or simply look at them. He can write the meaning on the card if he wishes to. He is alphabetizing, learning dictionary skills, building his own reference book.

You or a helper will type the stories every night and return them to be read aloud. Invariably, each student should read his story in printed form the second day. Some students may type their stories.

If a story is written every day, at the end of a month each student will have about 20 stories and perhaps 30 to 200 words on file. The notebook is his rough draft; the typed copy his final work.

Take some time out to have students put the typed copy in a booklet, make covers, illustrate the text, and review the words.

Look through the stories to see how much vocabulary is being learned and where other words must be taught.

If necessary, teach the basic sight words and use other techniques to show students how to sound out words, construct words, divide words.

Keep many books in the room on the subjects the students write about, since these are the things that interest them. They will read these books.

Before I discuss another reading method, let me tell you about an experience I had when I used this kinesthetic method with a group of boys in secondary school. Most of these students were interested in automobiles and usually wrote about them. After I had written a number of words on flash cards for one, he asked me to write the next one on the chalkboard for him. He was tired of sitting and tracing and wanted to stretch his legs. It was clear, too, that he no longer felt that tracing was for babies.

I wrote the word on the board, and he began to trace it with his finger, softly saying the syllables aloud. If you trace a word on the chalkboard, your finger will gradually erase the word. As this happened, the boy lighted up and really *yelled:*

"Mrs. Brooks, do you know what's happening? The word is going off the board, up my finger and arm to my brain."

"It certainly is," I said. "That's exactly what is happening."

The student wrote that word, and others soon joined him at the chalkboard, letting words go through their fingers, up their arms to their brains. Perhaps this is not what really happened, but if they thought so they were able to make it so. Emerson said, "As a man thinketh in his heart, so is he." I say, "As a student thinks he learns, so does he."

The next reading method may seem to you to be out of place in this book. I could have included it in the language section and called it a grammar lesson. But perhaps you agree with me that teaching grammar for its own sake to these students is inadequate and frequently pointless. It is better to find out what grammar they already know and use; then use language arts methods to strengthen what they know, to make them aware of how much they know, and to provide alternatives. Remember that they will use a new grammar only if they choose.

The next method can fit into any section of language arts. It can be called "living sentences" and is especially helpful to teachers who are not convinced that their students know English grammar. Students who do not speak English cannot be involved—at first—in the method, but they can watch and learn, and gradually they can be worked into it, especially if they learn best with their bodies. For this is a kinesthetic, movement-oriented learning process, too seldom used in our seat-bound classrooms. I will give the simple way first, then suggest possible alternatives. You can be really creative and think of other ways. You will need large flash cards, colored pens or pencils, and a chalkboard (and chalk) or an overhead projector (and transparencies).

Write a word on each flash card. The words you select must form a simple sentence. Choose an easy one first, like:

the / boy / ran / down / the / street

Shuffle the cards (or let a student do it), then pass them out to six students and ask them to stand in front of the class with the cards facing the class. Then ask someone to read the "sentence," which might be:

street / boy / the / down / the / ran

Even before you ask them to do so, your students will put the words in order. You may ask a student to move the cardholding students around to form a sentence. They will have formed a sentence without recourse to rules of grammar. Tell them so.

Give "tall" or another adjective to a student and ask him to place himself in the sentence. Give out other adjectives (without identifying them as such) and call attention to the fact that students will invariably place themselves before "boy" or "street." Let students supply adjectives.

Then pass out "slowly," or some other adverbs. (Depending on your class, this may be done on another day.) Again, students will rely on their already extensive knowledge of language patterns and place themselves properly into the "living" sentence.

You are ready now to use the chalkboard or overhead projector, or to let a student or aide do this. Write each word in your sentence at the head of a column, using only one adjective, like this:

The   tall   boy   ran   slowly   down   the   street

Ask questions like these:
Where should the other describing words go? (Then write them under "tall.")

Can "slowly" fit anywhere else? Show me. (You may want to ask for other words and test them.)

What can you use instead of "ran"? (Students may write on the flash cards and on the chalkboard.)

Can you separate the words "down the street"? (I usually give boys "down" and "street" and give a girl "the." When the class has agreed that these cannot be separated, I have them lock arms and, like "slowly," move to other slots in the sentence. This is fun.)

I ask them to give me other groups of words like "down the street." Because of what has just happened, there is usually a lot of enthusiasm here. Write these prepositional phrases on the chalkboard or transparency (but without using the term "prepositional phrase").

I need not go into this further, but you can add variations like these:

Use different colors for the different classes of words.

Have students make a question from the statement by giving out "did." They will see that "ran" must become "run." They may even notice that although no period was used, they need a question mark.

Let students replace your words with others.

Let students read the sentences aloud, singly or in chorus, emphasizing certain words to change sentence meaning.

With longer sentences, make groups of words to show how phrase reading is done.

Now see what else you can do with this method on your own. Remind students how much they do know about grammar. You are showing them what they know, building their confidence, using a teaching method that is best for the kinesthetic learner who learns through his body and through manipulation. And they are practicing simple but important reading skills. (The idea for this method comes from a demonstration by Bernard Weiss of Milwaukee.)

Listen and Read

Listen and read is a simple but often overlooked technique. Just read aloud to your students as they read silently, or let them listen to a story, poem, or ballad on a record player or a tape recorder. If you like, ask leading questions before your students begin the exercise, but ask "thinking" rather than "recalling" questions. Content from subjects such as history or science can be used, and even mathematics problems can be heard and read at the same time.

Whether we like it, parents and teachers of other subjects expect English teachers to help students read better in all content areas. We cannot escape this responsibility, so we may as well accept it gracefully and make it fun. Also, we may be discovering another learning style that can be exploited further as we move into reading literature.

If your school has listening posts or stations with earphones which can be plugged into jack boxes, you can individualize the listening, or group students in a number of different ways. Or use the cassette tape recorder, transparencies, slides, or filmstrips. There are even films designed for listening and reading activities. Or you may be able to work out an arrangement with the foreign language teacher for some use of the language laboratory. Use it with second language methods, but use it also for this kind of listening and reading activity.

For example, let us say you have an eighth or an eleventh grade class working with American studies, both English and history. If they have been studying the Civil War you might arrange to have them listen to "A Horseman in the Sky" by Ambrose Bierce. Some preliminary questions might be:

Did members of the same family ever fight on different sides in the Civil War? Can you prove this? Give examples? Could this have happened in other wars? American wars?

Then let them listen up to the point where the sergeant asks Druse if there was anybody on the horse. Stop reading or playing the story and ask: What do you think Druse will reply?

Go back to the story to find clues. (Students may listen again to the parts where he says farewell to his father, and to the moment, just before he fires, when he remembers that his father said, ". . . do what you conceive to be your duty." If you have reproduced the story, students may listen and read.)

What does the father mean?

What has this to do with this story? With this war? With any war?

Now play the end of the story and discuss it further.

This technique will help students get meaning from context, for many of the difficult words in the Bierce story are clearer when they are *heard* and *read* at the same time. It will help them to phrase better as they read, for they will be listening to a model. And don't worry if some don't read at all, but just listen. Use the method enough, encourage them, and they will read eventually.

To vary this method, and to keep students *reading,* occasionally read or record a word or phrase that is *not* in the original selection piece. Or leave some silent places. See how quickly they catch on. But don't make it a trap; make it fun.

Now see how many variations you can play on this theme, remembering that if you expect to be successful you must be creative and not merely do what I, or anyone else, tells you to do.

You will have some students who need help with the sounds letters make. Here again machines will help. The Language Master and Card Reader are designed so that you can create models for students to imitate. There are phonics games based on Bingo and Lotto which can be played, and you yourself can devise games with your students.

You can work through the phonics rules in an inductive way so that students discover for themselves the rules for the sounds made in forming English words. I strongly recommend avoiding elementary materials. Students resent being taught as though they were in elementary school, and your phonics instruction must be subtle.

Every secondary school teacher will want to know enough about developmental reading to do an informal reading inventory, teach a directed reading lesson, teach skimming and scanning techniques, and help students improve speed—and he should know when to refer a student for special help. Every prospective teacher should himself have gone through the process of taking several reading tests of the kinds secondary school students take, and being involved in the reading processes mentioned here. He should be familiar with some of the instructional materials for reading—charts, kits, films, tapes, records, workbooks, and machines—and be able to use them with his students and evaluate these materials.

Investigate the methods and materials discussed in this chapter. Don't stop with these suggestions; continue to investigate and use yourself as a guinea pig. If you cannot succeed with them, if you are turned off by such methods and materials, your students will be too. But if something excites and intrigues you and makes you want to learn, don't let it go. Use it as it is, or modify it and help your students learn.

4　Approaching Language Differences

Despite the fact that language instruction addresses itself to the most delicate and complex adjuncts to the nervous system, it has lent itself to some of the most aggressive and simplistic teaching methods conceivable. Notions of right and wrong, correct and incorrect, die a slow and painful death, if they die at all. If we are honest with our students, we will set the record straight at the beginning: correct English is important to know for reasons of economic gain, social comfort, and mobility. We should quickly dispel the myth that one language style is more intelligent than another. The problem, of course, does not disappear with this admission, but it will create a baseline of trust and truth from which effective instruction can develop. Still, we must do what we know will be vital in the student's life in the real world: get him to handle standard English so that he can speak it, write it, read it, and understand it when he hears it. But we must assure him (and remind ourselves) that a nonspeaker is not a nonthinker—or, to the point, a nonfeeler.

A flurry of new articles and publications are describing the ways people handle English. Different as many of the theses in these works are, they seem to have one thing in common: an attempt to get teachers of language instruction to let go of the language, to listen to it anew, and to allow it to change—to live. But even those of us who are already able to do this have the problem of what to do with the material. The world of print is represented, for the most part, in standard English—certainly the world of scholarship and instruction is. Now our problem is what to do with the student who does not, cannot, or will not abandon nonstandard English and accept standard English.

The best approaches to solving this problem are the second language methods. These approaches consist of teaching such students a second or "standard" English dialect, and teaching English as a second, or foreign, language to the Spanish speaking, to Hawaiians, to American Indians, and to others whose first language is a dialect or a foreign tongue. For us, this means facing a student body which is culturally different and often diverse because of language, race, color, or foreign birth. The realities of American schools make the Spanish language, the ghetto idiom, and the nonstandard dialects of many parts of the country barricades to successful learning experiences. It is our job as teachers to breach these barricades without destroying the student in the process.

What are the best possible conditions for learning? How can these conditions be applied to second language approaches in learning English? The answers to these questions will be found only partially in methodology and teaching materials. Primarily, the attitudes, expectations, and personality of the teacher count most in this sensitive field.

Thus the first and most important requirement is the formulation of a philosophy that will shape our approaches to teaching English as a second dialect or a second language. The core of this philosophy must make clear that there is no intent to reject the language and background of students because they are different. On the contrary, your guiding philosophy should be that students are bringing to their school a worthwhile language culture that has served ably in its own milieu. Their problem now is to adapt to a language which may provide ways to greater educational and career opportunities and which promises a less frustrating daily life in the United States. *Not* that knowing another language *defines* their intellect; it simply enhances it. It is to these factors that the student will respond and, in doing so, set the tone of the classroom.

Following a clarification of our philosophical position, we move into the learning environment (a new phrase for an old place: the classroom). By extension, the classroom/learning environment includes the electronic laboratory, the library, and the media center. The hub of these learning activities is the teacher. Although we cannot be more (or less) than human, we should hope that our personality includes the attributes of being fair, humane, resourceful, confident, and expectant of maximum achievement from all students. In the projection of the teacher's personality into the classroom, these qualities will find expression in a poised and personable physical appearance, an attractively arranged room, the hum and tone of activities which allow freedom and movement within orderly limits, and a relationship of mutual respect that will enable us and our students to work together. The objective of the learning environment must not be lost: we are helping students to learn a second dialect or a second language that is related to their daily lives and future hopes.

Let's begin with a new understanding of language—somewhat different from the description given earlier. By definition, language is a system of sounds set up in arbitrary patterns whose structure and assigned values convey meaning in a given culture. English, Japanese, French, and Swahili each have their system of arbitrary vocal symbols. To learn another culture's language we must relinquish, temporarily, our sound and syntax symbols, accept the sounds, lexicon, and structure of another, and through repeated practice attempt to acquire competence in their interpretation and usage. Although this is an informal definition of language, it brings us to the consideration of principles of language learning as applied to the secondary school classroom.

Second language approaches in learning English rely heavily on the audio-lingual techniques of the foreign language classroom. These techniques require sustained oral practice of verbal patterns within a meaningful context to learn structure and vocabulary. The procedure begins with listening (audio) to the structure of the target language and continues with imitation, repetition, and other oral (lingual) drills of graduated complexity led by the teacher, supplemented by taped recordings, and carried out by students chorally, in selected groups, and individually. The idea is to make the most useful language patterns a habitual part of an unconsciously internalized knowledge.

The emphasis in this approach is on listening and speaking practice, with reading and writing developing from the spoken language. We cannot go into linguistic detail here, but since most of us are neither linguists nor foreign language teachers we must rely on the fact that these techniques have developed from the recognition that the spoken language is primary in man and therefore takes precedence when language learning is the goal.

There are basically two second language approaches: standard English as a second dialect, and English as a second language. Since they are not alike, we must distinguish between these approaches to select the one most suitable for the class. Let us look first at the classroom for native-born speakers of nonstandard English.

Standard English as a Second Dialect

Classrooms that require this approach will be found mainly in large urban centers. Cities like Washington, D.C., New York, Chicago, and Detroit already have some programs in progress. The student composition of these classes is usually predominantly or totally black because of the realities of segregated living, the rural South, and the development of ghetto enclaves. Like other dialect speakers, black people have produced their own language idiom.

The first task will be to establish workable motivations for both the teacher and the class. A large part of the problem lies in the fact that the students already speak English. Social factors also intrude in the form of spoken or unspoken resentment toward an acculturation process that goes along with language learning and which, in this case, sets up "white standards" as the model for imitation. Questions of what is "standard" English inevitably arise in the mind and may hamper our adequacy; after all, there are several varieties of standard English.

What we must recognize is that the concept of one's culture emanates from the language used. Language is an extension of oneself into the surrounding environment: it defines the self, it connects the self with others and with objects, and it puts values on them; it communicates knowledge, emotions, aspirations; it is the medium of social and commercial communication—all done within the context of understanding one's own culture. Foreigners and their children coming to a new land can see the practicality of learning the language of their adopted land; native speakers of a nonstandard English may well resent the implications that *their* dialect and the culture it represents do not meet the standards of other English speakers born in the same land.

Almost all the available information on English as a second dialect is devoted to (1) mounting arguments for the *acceptability* of nonstandard English as a point of departure, as a separate but valid language, as a kind of poetry, and (2) the *description* of nonstandard English as spoken by black people and anyone else from other than middle-class America. Although the first object seems to me wholly admirable, the second one—the descriptive approach—is, I am convinced, pernicious. For this approach does the most damage (by being incomplete) to those who speak a so-called black English. The assumptions of descriptive linguistics are that the language of black students begins with slavery; that it is the kind of linguistic compromise one might expect from illiterate children trying to deal with a new tongue; that, like children, black people handle the language they hear with some uncertainty, some innovation, and some competence but, unlike children, never seem to develop linguistically. The fundamental error implicit in these assumptions is that the child who is learning a first language is learning it in a vacuum—he knows no other language—but American blacks came to this country with a language, contrary to what we may have been told, and they used the language they knew in adopting the language they had to learn. This is not a historical curio. It is important in dealing with these children to present and/or acknowledge the linguistic precedents for their speech. It is important that these children know that neither they nor their parents say "dis" instead of "this" because they are stupid, or childish, or whatever, but they say it for the same reason that an Italian learning English also says "dis": there is no "th" sound in either Italian or any of the eight families of African language. Of course they should learn the correct pronunciation of "this," but they should also know that "dis" has a logical reason for existing.

If we are asked questions like "I talks aw'right, don't I?" or "It English, ain't it?" or "Why I gunna change now?" our answers must be honest but knowledgeable. Of course he talks right; his language has served him well in his community and it represents his family, his people, himself. But has it worked out in a social studies class or a biology class when a paper or a report is due? Has his language supported him to his satisfaction in reading and interpreting *The Invisible Man, To Kill a Mockingbird,* or an article in the newspaper about his community that somebody told him he should read? What about job application letters, directions for filling out forms, or taking tests? Hopes for college?

We all know the correlation of language to achievement in all school subjects—the connection of oral speech skills to reading and writing skills that will be useful in history, science, problem solving, civics, and other classes.

There is no reason why these relationships cannot be discussed honestly with secondary school students. The search for identity with teenagers is most keen, and we can capitalize on it to help students achieve personally and practically. The point does not need to be labored. It simply introduces the context from which we and our students can proceed in good faith. It implies, of course, that our aim is not to eradicate the student's dialect, but rather to make him bidialectal whenever useful. His speech may develop into two separate dialects, or it may become a dialect blend. The student's choice will depend more on psychological factors, home community reinforcements, and his aims than on any conscious effort on the teacher's part.

The best scholarship in this area is just beginning to emerge, for, as mentioned, linguists are too content to describe only existing language rather than to acknowledge precedents for it. As teachers we must demand the latter approach and ferret out the information concerning it. Otherwise our attitude toward the language of these students will always be patronizing when it is not fiercely resentful. It may be a simple matter of accepting their language as not only theirs, not only meaningful, but finally as respectable, logical, and, most important, worthy of recognition.

The worth of a language should depend on its efficiency for the speaker and its heritage. The prejudices against black English—in spite of, even because of, the recent scholarship on the subject—are all but insurmountable. Chief among the sources for this prejudice is the assumption that a refusal to adopt (or an indifference toward adopting) another language is a clear indication of mental sluggishness; that ignorance of standard English, vocabulary, and sentence structure is ignorance itself. This is so despite the fact that American English is itself a dialect—a "corruption"—of earlier English, and that, for an outsider, learning black English presents the same problem to the learner as learning standard English presents to a speaker of black English, with one exception: there is no trampling of emotions, no assault on culture in the former.

The horrendous possibility of assault makes language instruction so delicate. We are frequently puzzled and often confounded as to the way to help students become efficient in handling standard English without casting aspersions on the language they do speak. And all the texts on the subject cannot help the student if the teacher has no means by which he can communicate his respect for the language style the student brings to class. The easiest way, although sometimes awkward and most often unsuccessful, is to speak the student's language with him. Generally this fails because it is not done with ease, but even if it is, it may miss its mark because the point is not the teacher's facility for learning another dialect but the student's motivation to be freed from the limitations of knowing only one. Those who champion a complete disregard for standard English, who recommend total communication in black dialect, are practicing reverse racism—a racism that would deny any options and alternatives in life and language—simply because it relieves them of the responsibility of doing their real work: opening doors, not closing them.

Speaking the dialect can earn the trust of students and can be a device for encouraging them to express themselves. But it will never satisfy them—not until law books, train schedules, physics texts, legal papers, want ads, contracts, and income tax forms are also written in their dialect. And only if we wish to keep certain information carefully out of their minds should we agree to confining all language instruction to study in the student's dialect. Until the rest of the world—business and academic—converts to nonstandard English, we must content ourselves with giving the student a realistic appreciation of, and information about, his language. But this is the information that is particularly lacking in our sources—information that harks back to the matter of respecting the heritage of one's language. What needs to be done is to provide the student with a clear understanding of the sources of his language. Not the "Don't say this, say this" approach, but an explanation of why he speaks the way he does. For guidance in this area it may be unwise to confine our research to descriptive linguistics.

The History of the English Language section of our language texts always has something missing, some addendum that really needs to be included: the history of how English has benefited from the contributions of non-English-speaking peoples. No, I don't mean the Latin words or the French words that have enriched our language, nor the Celtic, Gaelic, or Anglo-Saxon contributions. I do mean the Indian words, the Spanish words; but I am concerned here particularly with the marvelous shape English has taken in the mouths of black people. Such an addendum might read as follows: [1]

The varieties of English spoken by black people throughout the Western hemisphere ought to be entirely different. In fact, they are different, but only insofar as the vocabulary and life styles meeting the demands of geography and circumstance are different. The similarities are overwhelming. Invariably, black English, wherever spoken, has retained the stamp of an African mother tongue, and this stamp has contributed significantly to the language we all speak in this country. When one thinks of how impoverished American English would be without the contribution of black Americans, it becomes clear that the connotations of "cool" that Marshall McLuhan has explained, the songs that the young generation writes, and many of our freshest expressions would not even exist. Black English contains the structure, vocabulary, and mythology of Africa.

There are three great linguistic designs in Africa: Sudanic, Bantu, and Hamitic. Blacks from the American hemisphere come almost entirely from the first two families. The Sudanic family dominates a considerable part of the West African coast and embraces such languages as Twi, Ewe, Yoruba, Wolof, Temne, Mende, Mandingo, Ibo, Nupe, Efik, Mossi, Jukun, and Kanuri. Some Afro-Americans come from the lower Congo, which is Bantu-speaking, and the Bantu family accounts for a great part of the languages of east and central Africa. What

---

[1] For this section I am indebted to Ivan Van Certimer, who permitted free adaptation of his article "African Linguistic and Mythological Structure in the New World," in *Black Life & Culture in the United States,* Rhoda L. Goldstein, ed. (New York: Crowell, 1971). Reprinted by permission.

appeared to early Europeans as bewildering differences among the speech of tribes along the west coast (the focal area of the slave trade) were in reality local variations of a deep-structured similarity. Under the surface of differences were certain basic patterns—patterns which were to assert themselves like engineering blocks and architectural blueprints when it became necessary for the slaves to build a bridge of communication between the European and African tongues.

It has been said that the forms of English spoken by black people in America owe nothing to Africa at all; that, in fact, black forms of English are no different from English spoken by lower-class white groups and that all the nonstandard elements in black English can be traced to an earlier English used and dropped by American settlers or still partly in vogue among lower-class American whites. Strangely enough, this theory was advanced in America by linguists who thought they were doing black people a great favor. They were putting forward this theory of similarity between white and black dialect of Americans to prove that where language was concerned, blacks were no different from whites.

The latest myth about black English is that its use beyond a certain age indicates arrested development—a failure, a deficit. It sees the problems of learning and mastering standard English as related to a whole range of social problems: the disintegration or lack of family structure (although the nuclear family has never been indigenous to black peoples anywhere in the world), poor motivation, underdeveloped linguistic and cognitive abilities, and so on. In short, it views use of black English as a pathological phenomenon—as an illness to be cured rather than grounds for the examination of differences in historical perspective.

The major differences between the two families of language on the west coast of Africa were lexical. In sound and grammar systems they are remarkably similar. When, therefore, people from various African tribes and regions come together, they can, without any significant shift in basic phonology and syntactic structure, make use of the words from one or the other languages in order to communicate. Africans devised bridge-languages to carry them across considerable areas of territory. This kind of bridging process led to what linguists call "pidgin" languages. Pidginization is a process that occurs when a common language is needed for contact and trade.

The Portuguese were the first Europeans to trade with Africa. These Portuguese seagoing traders would have had to acquire a new language at each port of call—an impossible task. The Africans solved the problem for them by absorbing Portuguese words, casting them into African phonological and syntactical molds, reworking the language, and regularizing it anew to suit themselves. Black Portuguese became the world's first trade language. In fact, it became the first worldwide *lingua franca*. It was so effective as a means of communication, utilizing a minimum of linguistic rules to convey a meaning, that it was used also in China, India, and Japan. It came to the New World in the early sixteenth century when African workers arrived in Spanish and Portuguese colonies. It flourished on both sides of the Atlantic for two centuries, and then the Dutch ousted the Portuguese and black Dutch became the next major trade language of the world. It is interesting to note that white South Africans today speak a kind of black Dutch (although many of them would deny it); black Dutch was a major element in the development of Afrikaans.

Black French came along in the same way as the French moved into the world trade market. Black French is spoken today in all the French islands of the Caribbean. In Haiti and Mauritius this language is remarkably alike although they exist half a world apart and have never been in direct contact. Evidence like this from other black language variants makes it very clear that black linguistic forms in the New World have substantial relationships to African linguistic history and development. Black English emerged in the seventeenth century when the English gained power in the Atlantic and moved into Africa, establishing a fort on the Gold Coast. Black English, however, did not come about merely through the collision of English and the African languages. The earlier bridge-languages that the Africans had developed, especially black Portuguese, have had much to do with the development of black English. By the end of the eighteenth century, black English was established at a number of points along the West African coast from Gambia to Biafra. It was brought to the United States from Africa or Jamaica either by the original slaves or those who followed in the next 350 years. The evidence seems to suggest that black English did not originate here in isolated pockets. The similarities between its variants are so striking as to make it unlikely that they emerged as independent developments.

Black English originated largely in Africa rather than in the New World. Some Africans already knew this English when they came here, and the common colonial policy of mixing slaves of various tribal origins so that they could not converse and conspire with their compatriots in their own native tongues forced them to fall back on this common *lingua franca:* black English, which they used on the plantations of America and the British Caribbean.

Black English, of course, has undergone many changes, more in America (where the physical and cultural presence of whites has been massive) than in the Caribbean (where the dominant physical presence is black). Its most distinct form in America, comparable with Caribbean black English, is along the coastal areas of Georgia and South Carolina in the form of Gullah. It is only natural that over the centuries its vocabulary has taken in more and more Anglo-Saxon words and jettisoned more and more African words. But despite the eroding of black English, several African features are still present.

1.   The absence of gender in some forms of black English. In Jamaica, for example, "him" may refer to a man or a woman. Likewise in Gullah, " 'im" or "he" can mean "he" as well as "it." Recall the Tar Baby story: "Br'er Rabbit keeping on axing 'im, and de Tar Baby she keep on saying nothin'." This absence of gender is a feature of the Bantu languages.

2.   Another feature of Bantu which appears in black dialects is the absence of intransitive, or linking, verbs. For example, "He is black" is standard English, but "he black" is part of black English. "Who is he?" is standard English; "who he?" is black English.

3.   There is a distinction between second person singular (you) and second person plural (yuna) in Gullah which is found in the Krio language of Sierra Leone. In the Caribbean and the United States, the equivalent of this is "you" for singular and "you-all," "y'all," or "allya" (Caribbean) for plural.

4.   There is no obligatory marker in black English dialects for plural, plural possessive or third person singular verbs. Thus we hear "ten cent" (rather than "ten cents"), "teacher book" (not "teacher's book"), and "He work here" (not "He works here"). These omissions are not the result of sloppiness or simplification. They correspond to grammatical features in a number of African languages.

5.   The absence of the phoneme "th," for example, in black languages is matched by a corresponding absence of that sound in African languages.

6.   Another African feature of black English is the use of specific phrases to announce the beginning of sentences: "Look here," "dig," and others. These

introductory phrases have similar use in Wolof ("dega") and Swahili ("de" and "eh").

7. One of the most prevalent aspects of African grammatical features in black English is the peculiarity of the verb system. Verbs in West African languages and in the Bantu languages in East Africa seem to focus more on what might be called the "mode of action" rather than on the "time of action." African verbs are best thought of in terms of whether the action they indicate is habitual or completed, or conditional or obligatory, and so forth, rather than whether it is in the past, present, or future. The concept of time among the Bantu is perhaps the most complex and profound time concept of any culture—a feature that has left its mark upon black English. Thus, the sentence "Dat man, he be fishing," is a construction that has no equivalent in the English verb system. It does not mean the same thing as "Dat man fishing" or "Dat man, he fishing." It is not indicating a man in the act of fishing at a particular point of time but is speaking of a man who professionally or habitually fishes. It describes an action along a continuum of time. If the "be" is deleted from that sentence, then it reverts to the simple present tense.

A final section in this proposed addition to our language texts would concern the actual African vocabulary that has survived: the large group of words known as slang or vulgarisms—that part of the language normally thought of as used only by criminals and delinquents but which has roots in the mother tongues of Africa. The following article can serve to introduce us to the subject: [2]

Africans and their descendants formed the largest non-British group in the thirteen colonies and in the United States during the formative years of American language and culture. Forced immigration from Africa began in 1619, a year before the Mayflower, and continued for almost 250 years, the last Americans of African birth being still alive in the twentieth century.

The myth of white supremacy has for long prevented America from acknowledging its African heritage, but the time has come for American schoolchildren, both white and black, to study the African, as well as the European, contribution to the language and culture of their nation.

They need to look closely at the western half of Africa, from where over 10 percent of Americans trace their ancestry, and especially at the history and culture of the great medieval empire of Mali. The language of this empire, Mandingo, is still spoken through much of West Africa and was spoken, either as a first or second language, by a substantial number of African immigrants to the United States: not surprisingly, the influence of Mandingo can be clearly traced in the development of the American language.

The civilization of Mali included a rich musical culture based on an elaborate range of string, wind, and percussion instruments and on a long professional training for its musicians. This musical culture has survived in West Africa for at least a thousand years and, by its influence on American music, has enabled the United States to achieve an independence from European musical traditions and to pioneer new forms. A bitter aspect of the American slave trade is the fact that highly trained musicians and poets from West Africa must frequently have

---

[2] David Dalby, "Jazz, Jitter, and Jam," *The New York Times,* November 10, 1970. © 1970 by The New York Times Company. Reprinted by permission.

found themselves in the power of slave-owners less cultured and well educated than themselves.

Associated with the musical skills of West Africa are traditional skills in the use of language. While the Western world has cultivated the written word, Africa has cultivated the spoken word, so that by African standards white men frequently appear inarticulate. This important role of the spoken word is preserved among black Americans. Here we meet one of the ironies of the American situation, in which black schoolchildren, skillful speakers in their own environment, are often assessed as linguistically backward by white schoolteachers. Most Americans regard black speech as a deviant form of white American English, not realizing that black English has a longer history than American English itself. A black form of English, strongly influenced by Mandingo and other languages, became established as a trade-language on the West African coast from the sixteenth century. Several West Africans are known to have visited London to study English in 1554, ten years before Shakespeare was born.

Distinctive forms of black English have developed and survived on both sides of the Atlantic. Striking similarities reflect their common origin in West Africa. The effects of black English and West African languages on the development of American English have never been adequately studied.

Many well-known Americanisms are in fact Africanisms, "O.K." being a notable example. Attempts have been made to trace its origin in English, French, German, Finnish, Greek, and Choctaw, but "O.K." can be shown to derive from similar expressions in a number of West African languages, and to have been used in black Jamaican English more than 20 years before its use by whites in New England.

Over 80 Americanisms appear to have an African or probably African origin, including such items as: jazz, jitter and jitter-bug, hep (or hip) and hep-cat, banjo, boogie-woogie, rooty-toot, jam (as in jam-session), to jive, to tote, to goose, to hug someone, to lam (meaning to go), to dig (meaning to understand, appreciate), uh-huh and uh-uh (for yes and no), ofay and honkie (as names for white man), cocktail, guy, and bogus. Many such words are direct loan-words from Africa.

Black American expressions like "be with it," "do your thing" and "bad-mouth" (to talk badly about someone) are word-for-word translations from phrases used widely in West African languages, including Mandingo.

In the study of America's diverse heritage, increasing attention needs to be directed toward West Africa. In this respect, the current concern with Swahili in the United States represents a false trail, since the study of this East African language is no more relevant to black Americans than the study of Russian would be to Anglo-Saxon immigrants.

West African languages, such as Mandingo and Wolof, are of much greater relevance to America, and the aim of progressive educational programs in the United States should be to place the study of West African languages and cultures alongside the traditional study of Western European languages and cultures. Such programs would not only provide a more balanced view of the American heritage, but would also give young Americans a better understanding of human societies beyond the confines of the Western world.

Information like that contained in these two articles would unquestionably fascinate a black student and strengthen his ego. He would appreciate the efforts of any teacher who could provide for him means by which he understood his linguistic heritage and means by which he could make efficient transfers to standard English. As soon as he knows that his ancestors have made significant contributions to English—standard and nonstandard—as soon as he knows that his speech patterns are not the result of sloppy or deficient intellect, his whole attitude toward language is likely to improve. And there is a strong possibility that his whole attitude about learning itself will alter for the better. Teaching that is, to use a battered word, relevant is just this kind of thing: it allows the student to discover himself in the mass of information that we present to him.

Other motivational devices will win acceptance as well as excite interest and creativity. We can start by reading two kinds of poetry to the class: folk and formal poetry that has been written by black poets, or, for that matter, a white poet of dialect such as Robert Burns. For example, Sterling Brown's "Southern Road" or "Memphis Blues" or "The Ballad of Joe Meek" in folk dialect can be followed by his formal English "The Young Ones" or "Strong Men." Selections from James Weldon Johnson's *God's Trombones,* such as "The Creation," can be read in conjunction with the formal English "O Black and Unknown Bards." Langston Hughes offers many opportunities: "Bound No'th Blues" and "Mother to Son" compared to his formal English "The Negro Speaks of Rivers" or "I, Too." Paul Laurence Dunbar's "The Party" or "My Sort o' Man" can be read alongside the formal "Life" or "Compensation" or "Dawn." There are countless other examples that will allow students to savor the difference between formal English and dialect English and at the same time appreciate the value of both. That scholars and poets—men of importance—can and do acknowledge both kinds of English and use them at their discretion suggests to these students that they might do the same and benefit from it. You can then initiate discussions, questions, and answers directed toward the uses of language and the history of language, definitions of folk, formal, and dialect and reasons behind their development. This will stimulate thinking and create new concepts in the minds of students and will go a long way toward creating the readiness to learn. You can do more than this. Use biographies of these and other writers for developing interest and skills in the reading aspects of language learning. And with regard to writing, encourage students to try their hand at expressing themselves creatively by writing poems and stories that use either folk or formal idiom [3] or that shift back and forth as the student and the material determine.

Although the method for learning standard English as a second dialect uses the audio-lingual approach of the foreign language classroom, it does not rest solely on this technique. The audio-lingual approach is a first step for acquiring phonological (sound) and syntactical (sentence structure) control,

---

[3] The term "formal English," in reference to poetry, also suggests a name for the course that school systems could adopt. Such terms as "Standard English" or "Remedial English" don't quite say what we mean and connote a value judgment that has an alienating effect. Why not Formal English as an accredited course offered concurrently with English 10, 11, 12, American Literature, and whatever else is offered by a secondary school English department?

and the natural direction from this point must be toward reading and writing. Your immediate goal in the audio-lingual technique is to develop in your students habit-forming skills in the use of the most functional English structures which will later serve as a base for interpreting and communicating their ideas. Oral activities should include repetition drills and structure drills subdivided into substitution, expansion, question/answer, and transformation drills. An example of a substitution drill based on verb person and number changes will illustrate the technique. The drill can either follow your brief explanation of the structure under consideration in which you give all the correct forms, or the drill can be practiced first and the underlying principles can be reached inductively afterward. In either case, students must know what they're doing and what they're in the process of learning. Students are people, not parrots.

Teacher (or tape)	Students
My brother works here. *(Repeat)*	My brother works here.
I work downtown. *(Repeat)*	I work downtown.
He_____.	He works downtown.
My parents_____.	My parents work downtown.
You_____.	You work downtown.
She_____.	She works downtown.
They_____.	They work downtown.
Helen and Jean_____.	Helen and Jean work downtown.
My cousin and I_____.	My cousin and I work downtown.
I_____.	I work downtown.

Essentially the method involves guided imitation with the teacher—and later the tape—serving as a model so that the student learns to manipulate the sequences and patterns for control of the language structure. Listen carefully to students' repetitions, stopping them to correct errors. Hand signals for stopping and starting drills will be useful and will facilitate giving a variety of directions. Your concentration should be on *what* is said and not on long descriptions and explanations about how we go about saying it.

The object of the following substitution drill is to reinforce skill in handling past tense forms and to expand vocabulary. Sentences are designed to improve the pronunciation of practical school words.

Teacher: Where did my friend go? *Repeat.*
Students: She went to the school library.
to the nurse's office.
to the Student Council room.
to the principal's office.
to fill out some forms.
to make a telephone call.

You should break down the sequence of drill routines from choral response (the whole class) into small group responses, row by row, boys versus girls and individual responses. The ultimate goal is their correct use in free discussion that you guide at first. After oral practice, the sentences can be seen (on overhead projectors, or duplicated copies if not available in books), read, recited again, then copied for writing practice and for future use in the development of oral and written compositions.

Sustaining pace and interest are two major problems in the audio-lingual technique. The pace must be fast, the kinds of drills must change frequently, or interest will not be maintained for more than a few minutes of drill practice. Weaknesses come from monotonous repetitions that offer little challenge to the older student, and from their failure to provide adequate transferral devices for developing reading and writing skills. Another problem will be finding material, particularly for the secondary school level.

Despite drawbacks, a modified audio-lingual approach works where the need is repeated practice until the performance becomes habitual. Linguists say that the use of the possessive, the "s" in the singular present-tense verb, the formation of plurals, the use of contractions and negatives (especially with "do") are among our most troublesome structures. Effective use of oral drills will help students master these and similar demons of the English language. Good sense dictates that these drills must be laced with other things and that the timing must be fast and short. The following classroom activities are examples for a class working on the use of the possessive.

Oral Practice

This should take five to ten minutes, no more. Structure drills dealing with possessive nouns (This is *John's* book); possessive adjectives (*his* book, *my* book); possessive pronouns (his, mine, yours). These drills grow from simple imitation repetition to more complex structure drills.

Drills start by using your voice as model, but variations come from using tape recorders in the room, using the language laboratory if available, dividing the class into groups and allowing those who have difficulty to use Language Masters or Card Readers (teachers can make their own cards for the structure under consideration) and other electronic devices on the market. Without any of this hardware, you can supply variations by moving around the room, picking up and putting down objects, asking whose they are and requiring the correct answer. Students giving the correct response then address similar questions to their fellow students, pointing out other objects.

Reading Practice

This should take approximately twenty minutes. You can use commercial material or an expository paragraph you have written, duplicated and passed out to each student. The possessive is the major construction; for example, "John's New Transistor Radio" or "Your House and Mine."

The teacher reads aloud at first, students listen and follow in their text. On the first reading you pause to ask questions after each sentence that will elicit correct responses based on the context, along with the correct use of the possessive when required. In later readings the whole paragraph will be read before questions are asked. Furthermore, student reading of the paragraph will later replace the teacher's reading.

Oral résumés of the paragraph using the composite method at first—each student supplying a sentence toward the summary—should be followed by individual students summarizing the entire paragraph. These summaries can be placed, sentence by sentence, on the chalkboard or on the overhead projector for class reading.

Writing Practice

This should take fifteen to twenty minutes. It includes copying the structure drills, copying the oral summary sentences, and copying the correct answers to the questions from early writing drills. Exercises using commercial materials and workbooks can be used as long as enough time is given for the correction of this material within this same class time, using the overhead projector or sending students to the chalkboard. A variation is for you to read the title of a story or expository paragraph, pause and elicit from students the questions that the title arouses in them, write the questions for the class to see, read the material, ask the questions, have them answered orally, and then have students copy questions and answers.

The intent of writing practice is to advance students to writing their own paragraphs, stories, poems; but this should be strictly guided at first if the aim is formal English.

The most successful activities are not as tightly structured as the preceding sample may appear to be. There should not be a single lesson plan on the possessive unless it seems advisable. You can spread these and other activities over the period of a week, using one of the devices illustrated above during the first fifteen minutes of each class period for a reinforcement of the structure or the vocabulary under consideration. The rest of the class period can be spent on whatever unit of work you have decided on, whether it is reading "The Legend of Sleepy Hollow" or a unit on personal writing.

In addition to oral and written structure drills, the following suggestions should reveal the range of possibilities for learning reading, vocabulary, and writing in a well-coordinated second-dialect program.

Reading

Use multi-ethnic materials in books; display pictures and posters; and use films, filmstrips, transparencies, slide–tape presentations as background for stimulating interest among Afro-American, Puerto Rican, or other students you will have in these classes.

Use the daily press, television, and radio for discussions about how people cope with life. These discussions should precede reading both short stories and novels that deal with conflict and problems. Ask questions that stimulate discussion ("Is truth stranger than fiction?") to encourage students to compare literature with news events, soap operas, westerns, and with experiences in their communities and daily lives. This in turn leads to another kind of reading: current newspapers and magazines, the different skills involved, the goals sought, the critical approach necessary, and the satisfactions received.

Use mythology for increasing reading interest and reading skills, for showing related ties among all human beings, and for connecting the past with the present. Start with names used in the space program: Saturn, Mercury, and of course the lunar expedition's Apollo, and so forth. The names of planets and constellations offer a further introduction, as do the derivations of names of the days of the week. Class discussion of mythology and how it grows should be designed to lead into the reading of the myths of many people—Indian, Greek, Roman, African, ancient Mayan and Aztec, Pacific islander, Norse, Celtic. This can be closely coordinated with the work in literature, humanities, and composition taken up in later chapters.

Discuss living people—actors like Sidney Poitier—who have learned to shift from one dialect to another. Encourage students to read their autobiographies.

Vocabulary

Just one example of vocabulary instruction should suffice. Vocabulary should be related to the student's world, starting where he is. Let him know you've heard some of his expressions—"dig," "out of sight," "lame," "baby," "soul," or any others that might be current (for you!). If students can laugh and teach you newer expressions, so much the better. Find out from students what expressions have become dated. Admit to them some of the slang expressions of your school days, your community. Have a good laugh together.

Get students moving to the chalkboard, making lists of their vocabulary, and indicate the formal way of saying the same thing. Build lessons from this—spelling, word meaning, and usage.

Read short stories and poems that include what we describe as the vernacular as well as formal English. Read examples of business letters, government forms, employment forms, classified ads, all using their special terminology. Read selections from the Bible and from Shakespeare that demonstrate both the simplicity and the beauty of the English language. (Point out Shakespeare's shifts in diction.) From these and other sources, help students learn the richness and complexity of the English language; show them the way to increasing their word knowledge as a direct route to interpreting and using the language in any given situation. And give them chances to find their own examples.

Use role-playing and class skits for illustrating the varieties of vocabulary and where to use it, and the ability to shift from one kind to another. Tape some of these, or use the teletrainer, so students can hear themselves shift.

Writing

Any of the preceding reading and vocabulary suggestions lend themselves to written composition as a final step. Limit writing at the beginning of the year to copying and correcting previously practiced drills, to writing brief paragraphs dictated by you and corrected immediately, and to writing expository, descriptive, and brief autobiographical paragraphs that class members have decided to write, have discussed, and are willing to read aloud to their classmates.

Use a class newspaper for developing a variety of writing experiences: "happenings" in the school, cartoons and jokes, editorials and essays expressing points of view, short reviews of books read in class, fashion and food articles, letters to the editor, original stories and poems, even a few ads that would require responses by letter from class members. Whatever goes into the class paper will develop from writing activities in the classroom, giving realistic direction to the lessons. The paper might come out only twice during the year but should be distributed in the students' homes, in the community, and perhaps to other English classes in the building.

Writing skits for class-produced "television" programs may be based on any of the reading previously described. You may be able to videotape these. Movie making on the secondary school level is another possibility and would require writing scripts as a first step. These scripts can illustrate the varieties of language.

Testing

Announce tests in advance to remove the fear of testing from the minds of students and at the same time to assure a valid measurement of student progress. Students should be informed of the material to be covered in the tests, and in the case of a unit, midyear, or year-end test, you will need to devote one or more class periods to review prior to the test. Shorter tests that can be corrected immediately on the overhead projector or chalkboard with the class cooperating need to be given at regularly announced intervals.

Our aim in testing is not to catch students, or to fail them, but rather to help them measure their progress and assure them of step-by-step success in their ability to learn English. Kinds of testing will depend on the language area under consideration: speech, reading, writing, vocabulary, syntax.

Flexibility and student performance are of primary importance. Lecturing *about* a grammar structure or *about* a story will be less productive than having students actually perform a drill, write a dictation, role-play, dramatize a story, or helping students organize a panel designed to discuss an issue that arose from their reading of a dialect poem.

English as a Second Language

Whatever the original language a learner knows, the principles of acquiring a new language are based on the goals of understanding, speaking, reading, and writing, in that order. Lessons should also be designed to help you give insight into the culture of which the language is a part.

A second language program should concentrate on the elements that make up a language, the patterns of language learning, and the course content best adapted to achieving the stated goals.

The basic language elements exist for purposes of self-revelation, communication, and interpretation. In all languages, they consist of the following: nonverbal elements, a sound system (phonology), a structure system (grammar) which includes both morphology (forms of words and their functional changes) and syntax (sequence of words in relation to each other), and a vocabulary (lexicon) which makes use of the other two elements to convey meaning and culture.

The patterns of language development can be described in relation to two factors: the levels of learning, from elementary to advanced; and the movement of learning, from the familiar (the known, the ego-centered) to the unknown (the new and the more abstract). If you keep these factors in mind, you can avoid unnecessary frustrations in teaching a new, or foreign, language.

To clarify learning levels, bear in mind that courses should not be divided into grades but rather into levels representing the elementary, intermediate, and advanced stages of language learning. Level 1 is the elementary level, whether the student is in the twelfth grade but has just come from Cuba without knowing a word of English, or whether the student is in the eighth grade and has lived in the United States long enough to pick up a dialect. In any case, he can speak English haltingly but cannot read or write. The prevailing present practice is to allow two years in elementary and junior high schools for the completion of a single level, and one year in the high school grades for the completion of a level. In the case of second language learning in adult education classes, learning levels are more than likely condensed to six, eight, or twelve weeks. As a consequence, teaching a second language class usually means that the student body is more heterogeneous in grade and age span than a regular eleventh grade English class or a ninth grade biology class. Some schools, for funding and staff reasons, can offer only one second language English class in which you may find all those who must learn English as a foreign language. In adult education programs, ages in second language classes may range from 19 to 60 years.

Another variation in second language classes is that students may come from many different countries, each speaking his own language with little or no ability to communicate adequately outside that language. Even an apparently homogeneous class of Spanish speakers usually represents six or seven different countries. I know second language teachers who have had students in a single level 1 class coming from nine countries: Colombia, Guatemala, Cuba, Puerto Rico, Mexico, Spain, El Salvador, Brazil, and Chile. The two Brazilians spoke only Portuguese; the others spoke Spanish in a variety of ways and often argued back and forth over a word or an expression whose meaning was not the same in their respective countries.

Learning about students' backgrounds suggests a key to your using the movement from the known and familiar to the new as a pattern of language development. Rosa's case is an example.

Rosa was 15 years old and had been placed in the school just three weeks after she arrived from Guatemala. Everything was strange to her, and many things represented a threat: the noisy bus that brought her to school, the big building with more than a thousand students milling in its halls when the bell rang, the books written in English that were thrust into her hands, teachers lecturing in English, the signs, the lunch lines.

Some people were kind to her, others ignored her, but she shrank from contacts because she understood so little, because she was ashamed of being different, and because she was fearful of making a mistake. Her English class represented an oasis. Her teacher, Mrs. S——, knew only a few words of Spanish, but she was kind and seemed to enjoy having Rosa in the room. On the first day she consulted a paper, called Rosa to her desk (pronouncing her name a little strangely but saying it carefully so Rosa knew she was being addressed).

When Rosa reached the desk, Mrs. S—— pinned a small card on Rosa's sweater that had her name written on it, and the word "Guatemala." Mrs. S—— led her to a large map on the front board, speaking naturally what were apparently words of greeting. Mrs. S—— then pinned a tag with Rosa's name onto the outline of her country on the map. Pointing, Mrs. S—— said, "This is a map," encouraging Rosa to repeat several times "map, This is a map." Then Mrs. S—— asked the question, "What is this?" and by pointing and giving the answer got Rosa to say, "This is Guatemala." Rosa noticed that there were other names pinned onto other countries on the map, including another student's name pinned on Guatemala.

Directing Rosa to her seat, Mrs. S—— stood by her desk and said, "Class, this is Rosa. She's from Guatemala." The class responded, "Good morning, Rosa." Mrs. S—— started with the first row and asked a boy seated there: "Good morning. What's your name?" He answered, "Good morning, Mrs. S——. My name's Luis A——." The teacher asked, "Where are you from?" and Luis answered, "I'm from El Salvador." And so it went around the room, and Rosa understood what was going on. At last, in response to Mrs. S——'s question, Rosa was able to say, "Good morning. My name is Rosa P——, and I'm from Guatemala." Sitting at her desk and looking at her name flying over her country, Rosa felt that she *could* learn English.

The final consideration in the development of a program deals with course content. Much of the content will depend on the kind of textbook used. Although you are not likely to make final decisions or to institute immediate changes, you should know what characterizes a good text and how to use it. One or all of the following can be expected: the author's preface or introduction, a preliminary guide to teachers, and often an accompanying teacher's handbook. You should study each one thoroughly before planning your course and preparing your lessons.

Most texts now in use are designed to advance the goals of understanding, speaking, reading, and writing the target language. Lessons are introduced through dialogs, pictures, or a sequence of sentences based on a given topic. Pronunciation exercises and audio-lingual drills for expanding vocabulary and reinforcing sentence structures are based on the dialog material or topical sentences of each lesson. Usually after the first six to ten lessons, reading material is introduced that reworks the same vocabulary. Written work in the beginning is confined essentially to copying audio-lingual drills, filling blank spaces with the correct responses, and answering brief questions—all of which have been practiced orally first. Many second language textbooks have accompanying workbooks in which students are to write out exercises based on the lessons. This exercise is good provided it is carefully guided by the teacher and is corrected immediately at the board or with an overhead projector. Assigning workbook exercises as homework is unwise. Students tend to resort to peculiar and mysterious spellings (most closely aligned to the sound of their language), or they fail to follow directions or understand the questions. They laboriously copy out their mistakes, all of which must be undone by the teacher the next day.

Homework on the elementary level should be limited to memorizing the dialogs or sentences of the lesson and learning the drills already practiced in class. You can check homework by calling on individual students to recite lessons, respond to questions, or act out dialogs with textbooks closed. Homework on the intermediate and advanced levels will follow the same basic patterns as that of the elementary level but will be more advanced in choice of reading selections, writing exercises, and cultural material. You will find that textbooks on all levels will gradually increase the scope of assigned home lessons.

A valuable added feature will be the audiovisual materials that accompany most of the newer texts and make up interrelated learning units, often called learning packages. Thus each unit in the text has tapes that repeat the text material, films that highlight each topic, usually showing some cultural aspect, and records that may repeat the printed material or may—and often do—add songs or some literary presentation. Filmstrips accompanied by tapes, and slide–tape presentations are now available. The cassette now makes the tape recorder easy to use. For individualized instruction, listening centers may be available to you. Other adjuncts growing in popularity are "student records" which are to be taken home with the textbook for listening, repeated practice, and hence further reinforcement of the classroom lesson. The problem here may be that few schools can buy these records and give them to students; they must usually be purchased by the students, and although the cost is minimal, it may be beyond the means of a good many in the class.

In addition to tape recorders and film and slide projectors, many larger cities and some suburban communities can place at your disposal media centers or an instructional materials center, audiovisual libraries, and electronic language laboratories. All of these represent a useful expansion of the tapes and films and records that reinforce lessons. However, the basic essentials remain the same: your voice, the textbook, the chalkboard and bulletin board, maps, wall charts, and colorful pictures that can be cut out of magazines or borrowed from the public library. To these essentials I would strongly recommend for the classroom the addition of at least one tape recorder and an adequate supply of tapes, an overhead projector, and a record player.

If there is no language laboratory in the building, your request for tape recorders should be increased to at least six or eight, depending on the size of the classroom, so that they can be arranged on desks in one section of the room and thus serve as a useful mini-lab. At assigned intervals, a group of students could work in the classroom mini-lab, listening, repeating, and eventually recording the lesson while the rest of the class is engaged in a different activity under your supervision (writing their workbook exercises, for example).

Whatever tools are at the disposal of learners—from the traditional textbook to the most advanced electronic equipment—the construction of an effective second language course is your job. Its success will depend on assessment of goals, knowledge of basic language elements, use of patterns of learning most conducive to achieving the desired results, and use of the available learning equipment. The following description of a sample lesson sequence that has been used experimentally over a period of time may help you if you are going to be a second language teacher.

The First Day

When the class is settled in the room, call out the name of each student from the official class list; instruct students to respond with "present" or "here," and pass out name tags (written in advance) to be placed on the student's desk or pinned to his clothing. These tags will also include the student's country and will be used many times in subsequent lessons. Introduce yourself, using gestures to clarify (or pinning on a name tag), and have the class repeat your name before and after writing it on the chalkboard. Then proceed as follows:

Teacher: (Going to map and pointing) North America is a continent.
Repeat. (Gesture with mouth and hands to indicate that imitation of sounds
is asked for. The English word "repeat" will be of some help; it sounds like
what it means in several other languages.)
Class: North America is a continent.
Teacher: (Now use backward buildup to ensure correct pronunciation, word
grouping, and rising and falling inflections. Students repeat as directed.)
a continent. *Repeat.*
is a continent. *Repeat.*
America is a continent. *Repeat.*
North America is a continent. *Repeat.*

Use this technique throughout this and other lessons, whenever you think
it is advisable.

Teacher: (Pointing to Mexico) Mexico is in North America. *Repeat.*
Class: Mexico is in North America.
Teacher: It's a country. *Repeat.*
Class: It's a country.
Teacher: (Going to a student and pointing to name tag) Carlos is from Mexico.
Repeat.
Class: Carlos is from Mexico.
Teacher: (Going to a second student) Elena is from Ecuador. *Repeat.*
Class: Elena is from Ecuador.

The rest of the sentences in the lesson will be practiced in the same
manner, as you go back to the map and point in turn to each place and person
named. At all times you use normal conversational tone and speed and avoid
exaggerating any part of a word to clarify sound. Thus:

South America is a continent.
Ecuador is in South America.
Ecuador is a country.
It's a country. It's here.
Elena is from Ecuador.

This procedure is followed until within ten minutes of the end of the class
period. Pupils respond chorally, then by rows or groups, and individually as
you indicate with hand signals. Use the last ten minutes to write five of the
sentences of this lesson on the board or for an overhead projector so students
may see the sounds they have been making and practice them again after you.
They are not to write. Finally, pass out outline maps to each student with the
place names that have been practiced written on them. A final pronunciation
practice can be done using the individual outline maps, and you can ask
students to take the maps home, practice the words on them, and try to say

sentences they have learned in class about the maps. Drama and gestures—no matter how funny—invariably make the home lesson clear. An alternate wrap-up of the first lesson is for you to pass out duplicated copies of the first five sentences written on the chalkboard, asking students to learn and practice them aloud at home. Collect name tags at the end of the period.

The Second Day

The day's work starts with a résumé of the preceding lesson: rapidly paced repetitions of the same sentences, oral reading of the map words or the sentences assigned for homework, going to the classroom map and pointing to the places named, and so forth. The next step is questions and answers based on the lesson. For example:

Teacher: Is North America a continent?
Students: Yes, it is.
Teacher: Is Mexico a continent?
Students: No, it isn't.
Teacher: Is Carlos from Mexico?
Students: Yes, he is.

For a first question–answer practice, you give the correct answer and have students repeat. A variation is to give the answer first in the form of a statement: *Ecuador is a country;* then ask the question and have students repeat that statement as the answer. From *Yes* and *No* answers, questions should advance to *Where is Carlos from?* or *Where is North America?* and then move on to *Where are you from?, Where is Elena from?, Where is she from?,* and so forth. With promptings at first from you, the ability to participate in simple question–answer dialogs indicates the student's degree of lesson comprehension. This résumé of the preceding day's lesson should last no more than 10 to 15 minutes. The class should then be ready to proceed to the next step.

Pronunciation Practice

Now that students have English sentences to work with, vowel and consonant sounds must be isolated and practiced to assure a foundation of reliable English pronunciation. Later on diphthongs, special problem words, minimal pair words (rag–rack, bag–back) will be regular features of pronunciation drills. In all pronunciation exercises, as well as in dialog and sentence drills, you should concentrate on syllable stress, rhythm, and rising and falling English patterns. Use wall charts or pictures or material in textbooks, associating sounds with meaning whenever possible.

Set aside a special time for pronunciation practice each day, usually after the résumé and before tackling the new lesson. When available, use commercial pronunciation practice drills on tape to relieve your own voice. After pronunciation drill, the next step takes learners to the new lesson.

The New Lesson

With all books closed, all papers put away, the class can practice the dialog of Carlos and Elena meeting in the classroom:

Carlos: Hello, Elena. Where are you from?
Elena: I'm from Ecuador.
Carlos: What city are you from?
Elena: I'm from Quito, but I live with my family in Washington now.
Carlos: What street do you live on?
Elena: I live on Columbia Road. Where do you live?
Carlos: On Sixteenth Street with my family. We're from Mexico.

This sample dialog will be repeated by the class after you say it and practiced orally, just as the first day's lesson was developed. Thus:

Teacher: Hello, Elena. Where are you from? *Repeat.*
Class: Hello, Elena. Where are you from?
Teacher: I'm from Ecuador. *Repeat.*
Class: I'm from Ecuador.

This will continue until the dialog is completed. After its completion, you can develop variations such as the following: two students acting out the parts of Carlos and Elena; the substitution of other names and places for those used in dialog; students going to a map and pointing out places named; students answering direct questions about where they're from and where they now live; students answering questions about where their classmates are from by looking at name tags.

Reading

Pass out duplicated copies of a dialog (or have students open their books) for oral reading of what they have just practiced. Read the entire dialog first, then have students repeat it line by line. Next, your question after each sentence should elicit creditable answers; thus: *Where is Elena from? (She's from Ecuador.) Is Ecuador a city? (No, it isn't.) What city is she from? (She's from Quito.)*

At this point, you may teach students how to ask each other chain questions. You prompt: "Anna, ask Jack where he's from. *Say:* 'Jack, where are you from?'" (Or you can point to the first dialog as an example.) When Anna asks and Jack answers, it becomes Jack's turn to ask the question of another classmate.

Structure Drills

Drills from the first two lessons would be based on the following grammatical points:

> the verb *is*
> the use of *do* in questions
> contractions: it's, I'm, he's, she's, we're
> negatives: isn't
> the verb *live* (I live, he lives, you live)

Use the sentences in the first lesson and in the second lesson's dialog to form the basis for developing important speech patterns which are the foundation of grammatical principles. Insist that students go over these exercises in the language laboratory, at home, and in the classroom; and the ability to speak English will be developed.

Home Assignment

Tell students to practice and learn the dialog. They are to be able to answer questions and ask questions based on what Carlos and Elena are talking about.

Following Days

Start off each day's work with a résumé of the preceding lesson, with books closed and papers out of sight. Gradually lead students into conversations about the topic under study. This means they must learn to ask questions as well as to answer, and they must sustain a conversation by using the vocabulary they have learned.

Your breakdown of each day's lesson would resemble the following:

> Résumé (oral practice of assigned material with books closed; answering questions; developing sustained conversations)
> Pronunciation practice
> New lesson (including reading practice when it's part of the lesson)
> Structure drills
> Assignment

Writing

After several weeks, use writing practice to follow structure drills in the preceding line-up. Writing should cover the material already practiced orally or that is part of the reading lesson. Whether writing exercises are taken from textbooks, workbooks, or devised by you, they should be corrected as soon as possible in the classroom.

Vocabulary

To build up the learner's vocabulary, use textbook exercises, or those you develop, designed to increase students' stock of English words. Commercial flash cards, long used by foreign language teachers, can be used equally well in teaching English as a foreign language. Even better, use magazine illustrations for building up a classroom picture file that is grouped around topics such as the home, transportation, stores, family relationships, and so forth. You can use these pictures for eliciting name words, action words, colors, size relationships, and many other practical vocabulary items.

Another vocabulary stimulator involves your use of plastic objects that are found in dime stores and discount stores; for example, doll furniture, plastic fruit of every description, plastic flowers. Use of these objects allows students to come forward, to touch and hold in their hands the objects as they name them or talk about their size and color, or as they count them and practice addition, subtraction, and division with them. Still another vocabulary technique requires your keeping in the classroom a store of small household objects such as a tape measure, a yardstick, a hammer and nails, a clock, a calendar, a few dishes, a fingernail file, pins, pens and letter paper, keys. Naming these objects and using them for their intended purposes will go a long way toward fixing new vocabulary in students' minds. The use of tape measures, yardsticks, measuring cups, and similar objects gives you a chance to introduce the American metric system, weights, measures, and so forth. Such vocabulary practice allows for movement in the classroom and breaks the monotony that can develop from your strict adherence to daily schedules and assigned lessons.

Again you should remember that successful drills are flexible, rapidly paced, and changed often, for students grow restless with the monotony of too much repetition. Your use of films, slides, and the language laboratory will change pace and allow you to include cultural material while reinforcing the lesson. An important rule is that any material practiced in the language laboratory or on a classroom tape recorder must first be introduced by you in the classroom. Exercises are designed to help students learn important speech patterns. Going over them at first "live" in the classroom, then again and again in the laboratory (and even at home) enables students to gain control of the sounds of English, the sentence structure, and the grammatical principles on which the language operates.

Testing

Tests are available for second language learning, many of them accompanying textbooks. It is useful, however, to compose your own tests based on the material being covered. A good idea is to have short tests at least once a week which will help spot weaknesses in individual students, help both teacher and student assess progress, and serve as an incentive to learners to keep up with the material. Students should expect tests on a regularly announced day; surprise quizzes serve little purpose except to embarrass learners and to undermine their confidence in themselves and you. Such quizzes are disastrous in second language learning. Weekly tests should be brief and lend themselves to immediate correcting by you and learners *together*. Exchanging papers and using the chalkboard or overhead projector for writing the correct answers will be a learning experience in itself and at the same time will bring to light errors and misunderstandings about the material that has been covered during the week. Have students exchange papers at the completion of the test and sign their names with a colored marking pencil to the paper they are correcting, then indicate mistakes and omissions with a short line under each error. This gives a businesslike tone to the correcting period. Students do not grade their classmates; they simply total up errors and write at the top of the paper before returning the marking pencils to you and the papers to their owners. You can vary this by permitting students to correct their own papers, assess the grade (or you may eliminate grading), and by the next day return papers so that each student may correct his mistakes.

Give many types of tests. Oral tests require students to listen, record their responses to a question on tape, then listen to their taped voices as the teacher rates them. This does require a language laboratory, however, or a classroom tape recorder or a classroom mini-lab. In the case of recorders in the classroom, the rest of the class will have to be working on other material as you test a few students. The same technique can be used "live," as you call individual students to a desk or table in the back of the room where you listen to their responses to five or six questions or statements. In either case, oral tests should be used for pronunciation; for example, listening to minimal pair words and having students repeat them correctly. Oral tests are also useful for testing aural comprehension. Students are required to listen and make appropriate responses. Thus: *Thank you* requires *You're welcome; How are you?* requires *I'm fine* or *I don't feel well* or the like; or *Where are you from?* requires *I'm from . . .* , and so on. Each lesson should give you ample material for setting up this kind of test.

One good test is a weekly dictation of some 20 words which you can gradually increase. This combines both aural and writing skills. Read the material in units of complete sentences, allowing time for students to write the sentences as they hear and understand them. Such a test is an excellent index of the learner's ability to comprehend as well as his ability to write in English. This test, like all others, must be based on what has already been covered in class. Another test is an aural comprehension test over content material in the lessons. Questions such as *What street does Elena live on?* and *In what continent is Ecuador?* should require only one or two-word responses, whether oral or written.

To test structure, exercises for filling out blanks modeled after those in the lesson's structure drills are always serviceable provided students are not expected to perform too many mental activities in filling out a given blank. If you are testing their grasp of verb changes in person and number, the test should be limited to the tense under study. Learners should not have to decide between present and past tenses or between positions of the auxiliaries in questions and statements. To sum up, you must design tests to fit what can be reasonably expected of your students in the light of the work you have covered with them.

This has been a demonstration of the philosophical position from which learning English as a second dialect and as a second language should be approached. From this position you, the teacher, can originate your plans within the framework of good language learning concepts.

5

They Can Love Literature

There was a time when literature—if nothing else—belonged to the people: when whole villages stood around flatwagons and watched religious plays, or went to great arenas and heard the works of Sophocles, or to small stuffy theaters and listened to Shakespeare; when the most vivid and powerful epics were on the lips of every functional illiterate. Those days were depressing and uncomfortable in many ways, but surely one of the comforts—one of the reassurances—was the awareness of and participation in the literature of their country. One has to look to Africa and other so-called underdeveloped countries to find contemporary examples of this tradition in literature—a tradition denied to the populations of countries that followed the path directed by the industrial revolution. For with that event came first the commercialism and then the elitism of art. With the advent of printing it became possible and profitable to confine literature to a buying and reading public. Thus the death of oral literature, making many arts inaccessible to the young, the poor, and the illiterate. No longer was listening the one skill necessary for enjoying great literature.

It is natural and inevitable, then, that when confronted with the job of teaching the poor, the young, and those who do not read well, we return to the point at which literature was alive and responsive to the masses: oral literature.

Not only is the oral approach to literature a logical one, it is to be highly recommended on two other counts. First, it is an exceptional opportunity to share an experience with students—to be involved in an act of communication where both teacher and student are listeners or where the teacher can operate as the essential connection between the artist and the audience. This posture of a connecting link or an observing peer should be a comfortable one, decreasing tension and considerably humanizing the classroom atmosphere. Second, it is an approach made variable and exciting by the availability of so many media. No one teacher can read everything flawlessly, but no teacher need restrict his class by his own limitations in that area. There are records and tapes done by professionals of prose, poetry, folk songs, drama, and other art forms. Most recent literature anthologies come with supplementary material for listening pleasure, and there are any number of record-with-filmstrip combinations dealing with literature.

The important thing to remember in introducing literature orally is the participation feature. It is too easy to let the session begin as a listening experience and deteriorate into passivity. Once the students' attention has been gained, it must be kept by some activity on their part. Even in the most elementary listening situation—reading a story aloud—there should be some purposeful activity to follow. You might read a short story with a surprise ending and stop at a certain point to ask your students to invent possible endings. Stories which lend themselves to this kind of treatment are "Horseman in the Sky" by Ambrose Bierce, "The Sniper" by Liam O'Flaherty, "One Friday Morning" by Langston Hughes, "Cemetery Path" by Leonard Ross, "Dinner Party" by Mona Gardner, and "A Summer Tragedy" by Arna Bontemps.

If you wish to remove yourself from the spotlight, ask students to share favorite stories, poems, or books with each other in small groups. Rotate the groups so that everyone has a chance to share with many others.

Or, relieve both yourself and the class from the initial oration by inviting writers—including your friends—to visit your classes and talk about their writing and their writing experiences. These need not necessarily be professional people or even published writers. The point is to put your students in touch with literature as something alive, current, and accessible.

The title of this chapter says something about loving literature—that they *can* love it. Perhaps the phrase is misleading, for it suggests an ability your students are able to acquire; in fact, they already have this ability or have had it. In their years before school, they loved stories, rhymes, play acting—what they heard and what they made up. Our job is to recreate, stir up, that love of literature students once had and seem to have lost. Once we make the transition from exciting listening to exciting reading, the hardest part is done. Only two elements are necessary: curiosity on the part of the student and relevancy on the part of the literature. It is within our power to incite curiosity, to make a student want to know more about something—either by leaving out some vital information (for example, by not reading the surprise ending of a story) or by providing such a keen insight into a writer's work that the student wants to read more of it.

Relevancy—much abused as the term is—must be rescued from the dump heap of cliché terms to get at the problem of selecting materials. Relevant literature does not necessarily mean current literature; it means literature which contains the emotional depth and human behavior to which one can relate. Thus *Antigone*—the story of a teenage girl rebelling against the state as represented by her "establishment" uncle Creon—is relevant. So is the Book of Job—the story of a good man questioning the presence of evil and defying God to justify Himself. The world of good literature is read and reread because it is and has always been relevant. But there is no need to exclude contemporary literature from the realm of what is worthy—indeed, it is unwise to do so. The one thing that probably separates you from your students is a different awareness of time. For the young, the past is short; it is the future that looms large, and so it should be—otherwise they would be defeated by life before they had begun it. Reality to young people is the present. We accuse them of not considering the consequences of their actions when what they are doing is filling up the NOW space that surrounds them, and life lived this way is very intense. We should exploit that intensity—that energy—by directing it to a constantly creative exploration of contemporary literature evaluated in contemporary terms. The best rule to follow, then, is probably flexibility: a willingness to discover what they like, and what they are like; a determination to rely only partially on prescribed texts or notions of what must be taught. Do not limit students to anthologies or to courses of study which dictate what must be read. Fallible human beings prepare anthologies and courses of study —human beings who are often subject to community and business pressures. In short, their work is censored. Use anthologies and courses of study if you wish—your teaching style may demand this—but study yourself as you study your students to be sure that you are allowing yourself to develop as a teacher. Do the following things, even if you have to neglect others:

Read omnivorously, especially paperback books. Read mythology, folk tales, contemporary works, classics, poetry, multi-ethnic and adolescent literature. Haunt bookstores and libraries, sampling and reading.

Notice what your students are reading and read these works—whether you like them—to discover student interests. You may be able to suggest better works with the same themes.

Practice reading aloud so that you can share with your students. Include some dialect or foreign language in your reading, even if you do it badly. Let students correct you, and you will be employing the D.T.A. recommended earlier in this book.

Neglect (if you must):

Correcting papers. These students have already met enough red ink to drown in, and it is better to write a brief encouraging comment than to "bloody" a paper. Be honest; tell them you did not correct papers because you were reading something exciting. And then share what you read with them.

Preparing long useless plans. You must plan your lessons, of course, but you need not write pages of objectives (major and minor) and every word you intend to use. Let students help with the planning so that you and they know what to expect each day. Perhaps a prospective teacher in your class will write the plan with you or for you and even keep a file of your plans. Your whole object with your students is involvement, so involve them.

Keeping records which students are perfectly capable of keeping for themselves. For example, long book reports are a waste of time; let students keep a card file of books they have read. They may want to comment about the books to help a future reader. Let *them* keep class files or even individual files. Let students keep records of their grades, if you are going to grade.

You will think of other ways to relieve yourself of time-consuming duties which can be performed perfectly well by intelligent secondary school students. Teaching can even be done by students sometimes, if they have observed you and have learned to plan.

Black, Red, or Yellow Literature?

Briefly, before dealing at length with multi-ethnic literature, I want to explore with you the idea of responding to demands for the literature of one people only.

For many years the literature of this country has been almost entirely white. Except for those of us who attended black high schools, few English majors know much about the literature of races other than the white. Some courses in world literature do deal briefly with oriental literature, but few graduates of teacher training or liberal arts colleges know the literature of Africa or of black America. And even those of us who know black literature know nothing of others; we do not know oriental or Spanish American or Mexican or American Indian works.

Most teachers of literature have been—and some continue to be—disadvantaged in this sense and are therefore poorly prepared to work with students who now demand to know more about the literature of their people. Recently black students have been most vocal in demanding that black studies courses be taught and that African and Afro-American literature and language be included in black studies programs. Since this literature has been neglected for such a long time and since teachers are not now prepared to teach it, colleges and universities must begin to teach ethnic literature. At present, this probably means separate courses in non-Western literature which should be required for every prospective teacher.

Eventually, though, as all literature courses become multi-ethnic in schools and in colleges, and as textbooks begin to include the literature of the neglected minorities, the solely ethnic courses could become electives, to be chosen by those who have a particular reason for or interest in taking them.

Multi-Ethnic Materials

Suppose you are a prospective English teacher with a solid background of traditional literature behind you. You have been trained to teach *Macbeth, Silas Marner, The Legend of Sleepy Hollow,* and the American short story. Shakespeare and Tennyson, Hawthorne and Hemingway, Frost, Sandburg, and Emily Dickinson have shaped your reading tastes.

Now you have been told that the English curriculum is undergoing revision. You are informed that reading and composition will be approached from the multi-ethnic point of view, that the poetry and prose of America's cultural minorities must have an established position in the year's work. Aggrieved parents and students have demanded it; a beleaguered school board has ordered it. You, the teacher, must do the job.

What steps will you take to carry out this decision? What procedures can ensure a creditable performance? How will you start?

The first step involves knowledge: finding what is available in the field and selecting the materials that you can use. The second step requires action: lacing your course program, planning lessons and units of work with reading texts, literary, and audiovisual materials from a more diversified body of reading and writing activities than you have ever tried before. The third step deals with expectations: directing your knowledge and your course program toward what you hope to realize in the expanding concepts of learning English.

Acquiring knowledge about multi-ethnic materials is a giant step, and it starts with defining what we mean by the term. Within the educational context, "multi-ethnic" refers to the different racial groups and speech groups that make up the population of the United States. European Americans, Afro-Americans, and Spanish Americans represent three broad bands; Indian Americans, Oriental Americans, and Hawaiians, still another three. All of these groups can be more narrowly categorized into English, German, West Indian, Puerto Rican, Mexican, Jewish, Japanese, Chinese, and so forth. In the past, our teaching has been geared to the literary output of the English, with a bias toward European, or Western, civilization as the measure of educational and cultural attainment. It is reasonable, however, that the intellectual and literary accomplishments of other peoples should be brought into our classrooms. The omissions, misrepresentations, and stereotyping of the past must give way to a more realistic view of humanity.

English teachers are not expected to solve the social ills of a nation. Nevertheless, they can begin the process of educating all Americans to know and enjoy each other. Reading, written composition, and oral language activities all offer a route for introducing multi-ethnic materials in the classroom. Let us consider the kinds of materials that we will be learning to use.

Assembling Multi-Ethnic Materials

Folklore, fable, and myth.   In many secondary schools, a unit on myths and legends is taught in tenth grade. It's a good spot for introducing multi-ethnic materials. The more familiar myths are Greek and Roman; our job is to lead toward tales that other peoples have developed for explaining natural phenomena, traditional beliefs, and human behavior.

Folk tales, myths, and legends are brief; reading a few of them aloud to the class is a good way to hold attention and prepare the way for discussion. Collections of these tales from the neglected literature of other lands are appearing in bookstores and on publishers' lists. Teachers will have to judge whether this material will fit the class level they must deal with, but bear in mind that the outwardly simple folk literature of all cultures is man's sophisticated response to the human condition.

It would prove both interesting and profitable to play detective with the class, tracing a theme that appears in a particular story through the literatures of other lands, such as certain hero stories, sun god legends, or the Cinderella themes as they show up in various guises around the globe.

One book which might be added to the traditional classroom collection is *Stories from Africa*, retold by Shirley Goulden. Another, representing the West Indian tradition, is *The Iguana's Tail: Crick Crack Stories from the Caribbean* by Philip K. Sherlock, who grew up in Jamaica and heard many of these tales. The audience response to the traditional "Crick Crack" opening with the words "Break my back" suggests avenues of discussion that would uncover the varieties of American tradition in storytelling.

Stories in *The Three Wishes: A Collection of Puerto Rican Folk Tales* were selected and adapted by Ricardo E. Alegria and translated by Elizabeth Culbert. Twenty-two stories that have been kept alive orally for over four centuries are retold. We will recognize variants of some of these stories because they were brought to Puerto Rico by Spaniards, Mongolians, and Negroes. In *Tales from Old China*, Isabelle C. Chang retells ten fables and seven stories from that land.

For more information about materials, regularly consult booklists prepared by booksellers, publishers, libraries, and library associations. Pay particular attention to booklists of paperbacks. Students like their easy handling; schools find them financially feasible; teachers can use them to build up a broad body of reading materials for classroom shelves.

Short stories.   Everybody likes a good story. In making plans, choose reading material that represents a variety of ethnic backgrounds and experiences. Introduce this material the way you would any literary work to prospective readers: establish time, place, and people involved; discover the plot, theme, and motivations; evaluate style. Introduction of multi-ethnic material can fall naturally into a course outline wherever a theme, a literary period, or a literary genre suggests. Thus, wherever the short story of the nineteenth and twentieth centuries is under consideration, the works of Negro writers ought to be included.

One nineteenth century example is "The Goophered Grapevine" by Charles W. Chestnutt, which was accepted by the *Atlantic Monthly* in 1887. "Baxter's Procrustes" is another example of this black writer's work. Paul Laurence Dunbar, better known as a poet, also wrote short stories; one of his best is "The Lynching of Jube Benson."

There are many writers of the 1920s through the 1950s whose stories should be introduced into the English classroom. Suggested are: "A Summer Tragedy" by Arna Bontemps, "The City of Refuge" and "Common Meter" by Rudolph Fisher, "The Man Who Lived Underground" by Richard Wright, "The Homecoming" by Frank Yerby, "The Gilded Six-Bits" by Zora Neale Hurston, "The Boy Who Painted Christ Black" by John Henrik Clarke, "McDougal" and "A Matter of Time" by Frank London Brown, "Mama's Missionary Money" by Chester Himes, "And/Or" by Sterling Brown, "Karentha" and "Blood Burning Moon" by Jean Toomer, "In Darkness and Confusion" by Ann Petry.

Stories that deal with the Spanish speaking, the Indian, the non-Western cultures represent equally important components of the multi-ethnic approach. For example: *The Girl from Puerto Rico* by Hila Colman; *Indian Tales* by Jaime de Angulo; *Dark Side of the Moon,* stories by Phyllis Naylor; *The Battle of the 1,000 Slain and Other Stories* by C. Fayne Porter; *Jenny Kimura* by Betty Cavanna; *The Outsiders* by S. E. Hinton; *Tales and Stories for Black Folks* by Toni Cade Barber, and my own *The Outnumbered: Stories, Essays and Poems about Minority Groups.* Still another approach could use Pearl Buck's *Fourteen Stones* and Maureen Daly's *Twelve around the World.* The former deals with love and marriage in the East and West; the latter is a personal report on twelve young people and how they live (which stretches the definition of "short story" but leads to discussion, similar written activities, and perhaps original short stories based on "personal reports").

Poetry.   In dealing with the poetry of black Americans, the names and works of writers of stature need to become familiar to every English teacher, starting with poets such as James Weldon Johnson, Paul Laurence Dunbar, Langston Hughes, Sterling Brown, Melvin Tolson, Gwendolyn Brooks, and others.

If colonial literature in America is the topic of discussion in a high school classroom, there is no reason why the poetry of slaves Phillis Wheatley and Jupiter Hammon, and the later work of George Moses Horton should not be included.

In the 1920s came the Negro Renaissance, finding expression in the poetry of Arna Bontemps, Langston Hughes, Countee Cullen, Claude McKay, Fenton Johnson, Sterling Brown, and many more.

The sounds of the 1960s are heard in the published poetry of LeRoi Jones, A. B. Spellman, Don L. Lee, Charlie Cobb.

The poetry of other heretofore neglected groups in America also deserves discovery and dissemination. For example, poetry about the Indian is not difficult to find, but why not start with the records of a contemporary singer of her people's past and protests, Buffy Ste-Marie? Similarly, why not use the ballads and record albums of Appalachia to initiate a unit on the folklore and poetry of this neglected group of people? And if yours is a multi-ethnic group of students, let them try to compose poetry, protest songs, ballads that reflect their experiences and their past. The structure of poetry, the knowledge of literary genres so often confined in classrooms to the rote memorizing of rules and examples, can now become a genuine experience for students and teachers alike.

Biography and autobiography.   Slave narratives especially appeal to young people as a literary genre that is relevant to contemporary history and social questions. The authentic and moving narration, the simplicity of style, the passionate denunciation, even the majestic peroration of another age may attract those in our classrooms who have previously rebelled against other forms of literature.

Examples of this kind of writing include: *The Life of Olaudah Equiano, or Gustavus Vassa, the African,* written by himself, first published in 1789; *Slavery in the United States: A Narrative of the Life and Adventures of Charles Ball, a Black Man* by Charles Ball, 1836; *Narrative of William Wells Brown, a Fugitive Slave* by W. W. Brown, 1847; *Narrative of the Life of Henry Box Brown,* written by himself, 1851; *The New Man: Twenty-Nine Years a Slave, Twenty-Nine Years a Free Man* by Henry Bruce, 1895; *From Slavery to Affluence: Memoirs of R. Anderson, Ex-Slave* by Robert Anderson, 1927; *Steal Away: Stories of the Runaway Slaves* by Abraham Chapman.

Petitions, letters of protest, orations of black men during the slave era and afterward stand the test of time well and may be the essential instrument for "tuning in" many of the students in our English classrooms. Among the most outstanding is "Letter from Benjamin Banneker to the Sec'y. of State," 1792 (Banneker's petition to Thomas Jefferson deserves a place in any consideration of early American writing or study of nonfictional forms of writing). Others that merit similar consideration are David Walker's "Appeal" (an 1829 statement on black power), Henry Highland Garnet's "Call to Rebellion," 1843; and the cogent and moving latter-day classic, Martin Luther King, Jr.'s "Letter from a Birmingham Jail." In a class by itself is Nat Turner's *Confessions,* 1831, which could find a place in this group.

Biographies and autobiographies appeal to students because they deal with the lives of real men and women. Since most schools require them as a unit of study in the English classroom, this is an excellent opportunity to introduce students to the lives of men and women who represent a variety of backgrounds. *The Life and Times of Frederick Douglass,* an autobiography, illustrates a major work in this field. Others of equal merit should include Gordon Parks' *The Learning Tree* and *A Choice of Weapons; Coming of Age in Mississippi* by Ann Moody; *What Matter of Man: A Biography of Martin Luther King, Jr., 1929–1968* by Lerone Bennett, Jr.; *Nigger: An Autobiography* by Dick Gregory; *Thursday's Child* by Eartha Kitt; *There Was Once a Slave: The Heroic Story of Frederick Douglass* by Shirley Graham; *Black Is Best: The Riddle of Cassius Clay,* by Jack Olsen; *The Autobiography of Malcolm X* as told to Alex Haley; *Born with the Blues* by Perry Bradford, stories of pioneer blues singers and musicians; *Harriet Tubman, The Moses of Her People* by Sarah Bradford; *The Lonesome Road: The Story of the Negro in America* by

Saunders Redding, which traces the lives of 13 remarkable Negro Americans: Robert S. Abbott, Frederick Douglass, W. E. B. DuBois, Marcus Garvey, Joe Louis, Thurgood Marshall, Isaiah Montgomery, Daniel Payne, A. Philip Randolph, Paul Robeson, Sojourner Truth, Booker T. Washington, and Daniel Hale Williams; *Unsung Black Americans* by A. Philip Randolph; *The Making of an Afro-American: Martin Robinson Delany, 1812–1885* by Dorothy Sterling.

Moving away from the experiences of black Americans, we need to include such works as *Mountain Wolf Woman, Sister of Crashing Thunder: The Autobiography of a Winnebago Indian,* edited by Nancy O. Lurie; *Son of Old Man Hat: A Navaho Autobiography,* edited by Left Handed and Walter Dyk; *Down These Mean Streets* by Piri Thomas; *East River* by Sholem Asch, which makes interesting reading of Jewish and Irish immigrant families as they seek to survive on New York's East Side; *My Several Worlds* by Pearl Buck, which tells the true story of a woman who spent the first part of her life in China and the last part in America. Daniel K. Inouye's *Journey to Washington* is the autobiography of the first Japanese American to become a United States Senator from Hawaii. Moss Hart's *Act One* represents the theatrical world and is a famous playwright's autobiography, which goes back to his boyhood in the then predominantly Jewish Bronx. Oscar Lewis' *La Vida* could be included in this category; and his *The Children of Sanchez,* in which each member of a family in Mexico City tells about his life and his efforts to deal with urban poverty, is equally appropriate. *Chinatown Family* by Lin Yutang tells how the old blends with the new as a family makes its way in America.

Novels.   Major novels by and about black Americans should include Richard Wright, Ralph Ellison, Margaret Walker, Jean Toomer, James Baldwin, Ann Petry, William Attaway, Zora Neale Hurston, James Weldon Johnson, William Denby, and others of their stature. Teachers will need to be selective about the works of these and other writers, but experience indicates that young people will read what they want to read, once introduced to an author they like.

Works of fiction worth investigating include: *The Cool Cottontail* by John Ball, which continues the adventures of black detective Virgil Tibbs of *In the Heat of the Night; Letter from Peking* by Pearl Buck, in which the Caucasian wife of a half-Chinese, half-Caucasian man must help her son overcome his shame about his Chinese heritage; *The Chosen* by Chaim Potok, which tells the story of two Jewish youths who reflect the differing religious approaches of their community. *Cry, the Beloved Country* by Alan Paton and *Things Fall Apart* by Chinua Achebe are both extraordinary novels from and about Africa. *To Sir, With Love* by E. R. Braithewaite takes us to England for still another perspective on human relations.

Drama.   Most of us enjoy plays and the theater, and so will our students if given a chance. Don't limit class activities to scene-by-scene home assignment readings, class analyses and explications, or to just writing answers to questions. Open up the drama to the oral reading of roles during the class period, to creative role playing of a particular scene as the students see it, to making up and enacting a different ending before the class, to "reading" the play as for a radio show or a television rehearsal, to scrambled-role class reading (the timid student plays an aggressive role, the white student takes the Spanish American role, or the Oriental student plays a Negro role).

In addition to hilarity and fun, refreshing new insights can come through this route, and a genuine liking for good theater can be developed. Suggested titles in the multi-ethnic field include the following: *A Raisin in the Sun* by Lorraine Hansberry, *In White America* by Martin Duberman, *Take a Giant Step,* by Louis Stanford Peterson, *Five Plays* by Langston Hughes, *Purlie Victorious* by Ossie Davis, *The Human Comedy* by William Saroyan, *The Dutchman* by LeRoi Jones, *Blues for Mr. Charlie* by James Baldwin, *The Emperor Jones* by Eugene O'Neill, *Ceremonies in Dark Old Men* by Lonnie Elder, *Simply Heavenly* by Langston Hughes, *The Blood Knot* by Athol Fugard, and the marvelous and powerful plays of Wole Soyinka and John Pepper Clark.

Audiovisual materials.   An important adjunct to reading is the audiovisual field, in which films, slides, classroom display pictures, art prints by artists of all ethnic origins, and records and tapes—especially of ballads, folk songs, spirituals, poetry recitations, and dramatic presentations—will reinforce the classroom program.

The teacher's job is most important in orienting students toward the materials and in following up what they have seen and heard. Placing multi-ethnic pictures around the room, seeing a film, listening to a tape, is not enough in itself. It is the teacher who can guide students toward pleasurable expectations about the material, who can stimulate discussions, who can raise points, who can focus on a theme, and who can then channel all of these activities into creative writing and more reading.

A word about where to use multi-ethnic materials is in order here. Don't limit this material only to classrooms that contain cultural minorities. In other words, dismiss the concept that black literature is for black students only, Puerto Rican stories for Puerto Ricans, and so forth. White American students need to read about people other than themselves. They need to be exposed to the full spectrum of human intellect and activity. Besides being good reading, such literature gives exposure that will enable them to put themselves into realistic perspective with the rest of the world.

In every classroom the inclusion of multi-ethnic materials will begin to teach new and important facts about all people. Black students in particular will begin to see themselves *in* and as *part of* America. Pride and self-esteem are the desired bonuses. And the use of previously unrecognized literature, instead of representing preferential treatment, marks a healthy step in broadening education.

Constructing the Course

Knowledge of materials and the acquisition of those that meet the needs of the grade and the course under consideration lead inevitably to the question: How can we effectively use what we have?

Enlarging students' experiences through the use of multi-ethnic materials offers a variety of opportunities to develop oral and written skills in communication and interpretation. Achieving these objectives means that we must constantly refuel. We must first experiment with ideas; second, browse and study (in bookstores, libraries, at publishers' exhibitions); third, consult educational references; and fourth, be on the look-out for new sources of materials not necessarily on educational lists (a commercial film, a good paperback book, a magazine article, newspapers, a television program). Thus reinforced, we can begin to plan a program. A few random examples will indicate possibilities:

1. Have students read and share, through imaginary interviews, dramatics, and role-playing, some stories which portray personal development. (Use "The Homecoming" by Frank Yerby; *Autobiography of Malcolm X; The Girl from Puerto Rico* by Hila Colman; *Go Tell It on the Mountain* by James Baldwin; *The Chosen* by Chaim Potok; "McDougal" by Frank L. Brown; and biographies of Lou Gehrig, Jackie Robinson, Sammy Davis, Jr., Julius Rosenwalk, Frederick Douglass, Eleanor Roosevelt, Charles Drew, or Martin Delaney.)

2. Have a class project that traces the literature of America as it reflects its people: their customs, values, and the social and economic conditions of the times. Reading selections could be taken from Mark Twain, slave narratives, Walt Whitman, Langston Hughes, Bret Harte, Oscar Lewis, Richard Wright, Martin Luther King, Jr., or William Saroyan. Oral and written reports and a class bulletin board can be developed to illustrate this focus.

3. Have the class study meanings and spellings of such words as "stereotype," "scapegoat," "prejudice," "propaganda," "discrimination," "human rights." Use examples from literature to illustrate these concepts.

4. Bring in both the school and the public library as partners in acquiring more multi-ethnic reading materials and display pictures. Encourage students to arrange for exhibits and special programs based on material under study in the classroom.

And always, in following your English course outline, expand it to include multi-ethnic material as integral to whatever topic, literary genre, language skill, or reading activity is called for. Thus, if poetry is under consideration, include the poetry of cultural minorities which in the past has been omitted from the English curriculum. In the same manner, if written compositions are being developed, let students choose topics dealing with experiences from their backgrounds. In fact, *encourage* students to dip into their rich cultural past or into their impressions about adjusting to new patterns of living.

The unit which follows is offered as a further illustration of what can be done in the classroom. It is taken from an experimental curriculum on "Neglected Literature" developed by the Department of English of the Washington, D.C., Public Schools.[1] It may provide some ideas for developing other curricula of your own.

English Curriculum—Neglected Literature—Drama

A Raisin in the Sun
Lorraine Hansberry

Introduction.   Use of introductory materials in the text is suggested.

Play.   *A Raisin in the Sun* by Lorraine Hansberry. This is the story of a Negro family in southside Chicago. It revolves around the decision of the family to use a sizable sum of insurance money for improving their status. The conflict occurs when three of the family members assert ideas about how the money should be spent. These conflicts also allow for insights into each family member's personality.

Suggested procedure.   Read "A Dream Deferred," the poem by Langston Hughes. If required, have students look up the word "deferred." Point out after the analysis of the poem what significance there is in the phrase "a raisin in the sun," and discuss further the ideas around other delayed dreams (specifically, as related to the play). After the play has been read, refer once more to the introductory poem with such questions as:

1. What dream does the Younger family have?
2. Can you relate "dry up like a raisin in the sun" to the content of the story?
3. How is Walter Lee Younger's dream deferred?

Suggested questions for Act I

1. Describe the Younger apartment.
2. How soon do you realize that the Younger family is expecting something?
3. Are there conflicts within the family? Explain.
4. Who is obviously the head of the Younger household? Give examples to support your answer.
5. Find the dialog that shows Walter Lee's complaint against the women of his race. Is his complaint about them justified? Why or why not?
6. Discuss the relationship between Walter Lee and his sister Beneatha.
7. The end of the act in a play always has special significance. Why does the author choose to have Mama Younger tell Walter about Ruth's intention to destroy the expected baby?

---

[1] An Experimental Curriculum Resource Bulletin for Secondary Schools: *Neglected Literature* (Washington, D.C.: Department of English, n.d.), pp. 31–37. Curriculum chairman: Mrs. Rosemary C. Wilson. Curriculum writers: Lovelle W. Golden, Beverly H. Hyman, Lloyd D. Mayfield.

Suggested questions for Act II

1. What reason can you give for Walter and Beneatha's "back to Africa" caper?

2. What is your impression of George Murchison? Compare him to Asagai.

3. How does Walter Lee's preoccupation with the insurance money further affect his relationship with his wife?

4. Is Walter Lee being *totally* selfish by openly disapproving of his mother's buying the house?

5. Analyze the dialog between Walter Lee and his mother at the end of Scene I.

6. Can you justify Walter's drinking spree after his realization of how the money *will* be used?

7. Why would the family joke to Mama Younger about Mr. Linder's visit? Was it a serious implication?

8. How soon do you understand the purpose of Mr. Linder's visit? What clues are given?

9. Do Walter's drinking sprees prompt Mama Younger to hand over the balance of the money to her son?

10. Defend or oppose the following statement: Walter Lee Younger was not truly ready for the responsibility of handling the family's insurance money. It was obvious that his desperation to open a business was just that—desperation. He gave no real thought to the people with whom he was to do business, nor did he give any thought to the needs of his family. Therefore, the loss of the money (by way of Will's untrustworthiness) was what Walter Lee Younger deserved.

Suggested questions for Act III

1. Contrast and compare the backgrounds of Beneatha and Asagai.

2. Comment on Beneatha's anti-assimilationism and her confusion about returning to Africa when she is given the opportunity to do so.

3. Discuss the "backward step" in the thinking of Beneatha, Mama Younger, and Walter as a result of the loss of the money. Find the dialogs.

4. In the midst of this defeat, Ruth is the only character with any sign of hope and determination. Comment on this in terms of her situation in the first act.

5. Who or what makes Walter Lee change his mind about moving into Clyborne Park? Is it important to him?

6. Can you sympathize with Walter Lee's struggle to get his thoughts over to Mr. Linder? If not, why not?

7. Is the sister–brother conflict between Beneatha and Walter Lee resolved?

Questions on the play as a whole.   These questions should be under two headings: (1) Understanding the Play, and (2) Appreciation of the Play. Under "Understanding," questions should be constructed to get facts from the student and to develop further reading skills. Questions under "Appreciation" should deal with social implications and individual motivations as they relate to the play and as the play relates to human experience. Examples of points to be stressed under "Appreciation":

1. The matriarchal family pattern which is typical of many Negro families.
2. Walter's inner struggle to become a "man."
3. Mama Younger's realization of Walter's need to become head of the house.
4. Beneatha's preoccupation with nonassimilation.
5. The symbolism of the African student, Asagai.
6. Subtle discrimination shown by the representatives from the Clyborne Park Improvement Association.
7. The rightness of the Youngers' decision to move into Clyborne Park.
8. Speculation as to how the Younger family fared in the all-white neighborhood.
9. Application of introductory information (text) to the play as an art form.

Suggested follow-up activities

1. Voting on the most moving scenes in the play; assigning parts for acting.
2. A written character analysis of one of the major characters.
3. Investigations and reports on other plays by Negro playwrights.
4. The works of Negro musicians and artists.

Another play by Lorraine Hansberry is *The Sign in Sidney Brustein's Window.* This play is recommended for advanced high school students. The plot concerns young people who are "turned around" by the current events of the 1960s. The theme is idealism versus the reality of contemporary society. Note that this play is by a Negro but has no Negro characters. Miss Hansberry attempts to deal with a universal problem rather than a racial one.

For mature high school students:

1. James Baldwin, *Blues for Mr. Charlie*
2. LeRoi Jones, *The Dutchman*
3. Langston Hughes, *Simply Heavenly*
4. Eugene O'Neill, *The Emperor Jones*

For average (reading level and maturity) students:

1. Ossie Davis, *Purlie Victorious*
2. Langston Hughes, *Five Plays by Langston Hughes*
3. William Robin, *The Anger of One Young Man*

Expanding Concepts

Introducing multi-ethnic materials into the classroom means using books and audiovisual materials for expanding our sensitivity to human beings and human relationships. Through these media we share the experiences of other human beings in circumstances that are sometimes different from and sometimes like our own. We sense what it is like to be someone else; we feel the impact of that person's conflicts, predicaments, successes, and failures. By making a deliberate effort to use multi-ethnic materials, we free ourselves and our students from stereotypes and misleading myths, and we begin to identify with all members of the human family. These, at any rate, are our expectations.

6

Meshing Reading and Literature

Just as students resent attacks on their language and reject demands that they change it, so also do they reject a diet of literature "for their own good" chosen by someone else. Some of the affronts to students in this respect are a recitative of pain.

A boy from rural Mississippi is asked to read *Vanity Fair; Pride and Prejudice* is assigned to a girl from the slums of Chicago. Neither is prepared for these books' setting, mood, or tone, let alone their vocabularies.

Immigrants speaking little or no English are given books that are absolutely unintelligible to them. Big, thick books full of stories and poems about strange people and written in a strange language can make them dislike literature and everything else about English.

Users of nonstandard English are kept unaware of dialect poetry which reinforces their love of their language and through which they might be led to an interest in standard English poems. Instead, they too must go into the lockstep curriculum, with certain works read by everyone for some perhaps once reasonable purpose.

People with a non-Western cultural heritage are expected to concentrate on works of Western literature, as though Africa and Asia did not exist, as though there were no American Indians or Afro-Americans.

Middle-class students alienated from the mainstream culture are not permitted to read and discuss in school the books they see in bookstores and in magazines: *Huckleberry Finn, Catcher in the Rye, Black Boy.* They see quite clearly that school is not real and that their teachers have no intention of facing reality with them.

Those students whose learning style is slow are given too much, too quickly. Those who are really retarded learners and do not read well are not permitted access to literature in other ways: aurally or visually, for example.

Too many are kept from literature in which they can see themselves or others like them. They do not encounter the great ideas in literature. Often they are taught American and British literature in chronological sequence or in precisely the way the anthology is organized.

What can be done to take the dread out of literature study? First of all, we must become and remain constant readers of not only the great works in literature, the contemporary classics, and the usual adolescent literature, but also the little known works which will speak directly to students.

The Alienated Student

He is the person—quite often a boy in his teens, but sometimes a girl—who has never enjoyed literature or who has, because of inadequate teaching and inappropriate materials, been turned against it. He does not read well, believes that he cannot read well, has convinced himself that he does not want to read, and therefore neither reads nor enjoys literature.

Reading, for this alienated person, is another country—a strange land he travels at his own risk. He is Ulysses or Christian or Gulliver—even Don Quixote meeting a new threat with every new symbol in this strange land of the written word. Unlike these travelers, though, he has no hope of success. He expects to fail; others often assure him that he will fail. After a while he has been so effectively persuaded that he will fail that he often goes into a literature lesson *intending* to fail. And, of course, he does. In failure alone is he successful.

What kind of program can reclaim this alienated student? A program designed to capture his interest, to assure success, and to convince him of his ability to read and to enjoy; a program carefully planned to take him step by step through those skills which will make him a successful reader and a person who enjoys and understands literature; a program based on good and relevant literature that does not talk down to him but reveals and enhances his secret world, the real worlds of others, and the unknown worlds created through the inspired imaginations of great artists and writers. A program that is to have any hope of success with the alienated reader must take into account the failures of the past in dealing with him. And the program must have such impact that it will reach this reader and lead him into the world of books. The program's first potential failure is the failure to *see* the alienated student as he is, to know him, and to call his name clearly.

A First Question

Who is he?

He is the student who has not learned to read well or at all because of economic or educational barriers.

He is the student who does not live in a book-filled home, has not been read to in early childhood, and has not developed the habit of going to the library.

He is the student whose teachers have turned him against reading by too much emphasis on mechanical skills, the use of immature or boring material, or insistence on "correct pronunciation."

He is the student who hates books because he has no reason to love them. Books have brought him only humiliation and pain.

He is the student with physical, emotional, or mental limitations who must be taught to read in totally different—sometimes nonverbal—ways.

A Second Question

How can we improve the literary skills of this student? First, here is how we can *not* do it.

We can *not* use the same trite, poorly written, so-called teenage material that is supposed to interest this student—and does not.

We can *not* turn him over to the least well-prepared teachers, or the strict ones who will keep him quiet and in his seat filling in blanks—and learning nothing.

We can *not* assume that he is slow and simply unable to comprehend, nor can we assume that he will never be interested in enjoying literature.

We *can* not, we *dare* not, we *must* not give up. What can we do, then?

Bill Hull once said, "If we taught children to speak, they'd never learn." [1] I thought at first he was joking. By now I realize that it is an important truth. Suppose we decided that we had to teach children to speak. How would we go about it? First, some committee of experts would analyze speech and break it down into a number of separate "speech skills." We would probably say that, since speech is made up of sounds, a child must be taught to make all the sounds of his language before he can be taught to speak the language itself. Doubtless we would list these sounds, easiest and commonest ones first, harder and rarer ones next. Then we would begin to teach infants these sounds, working our way down the list. Perhaps, not to confuse the child—"confuse" is an evil word to many educators—we would not let the child hear much ordinary speech but would only expose him to the sounds we were trying to teach.

Along with our sound list, we would have a syllable list and a word list.

When the child had learned to make all the sounds on the sound list, we would begin to teach him to combine the sounds into syllables. When he could say all the syllables on the syllable list, we would begin to teach him the words on our word list. At the same time, we would teach him the rules of grammar, by means of which he could combine these newly learned words into sentences. Everything would be planned with nothing left to chance; there would be plenty of drill, review, and tests to make sure that he had not forgotten anything.

Suppose we tried to do this; what would happen? Quite simply, most

---

[1] In John Holt, *How Children Learn* (New York: Pitman Publishing Corp., 1969).

children would become baffled, discouraged, humiliated, and fearful; they would stop trying to do what we asked them. If, outside our classes, they lived a normal infant's life, many of them would probably ignore our teaching and learn to speak on their own. If not—if our control of their lives was complete (the dream of too many educators)—they would take refuge in deliberate failure and silence, as so many of them do when the subject is reading—and reading literature at that.

What can you do to improve these students' literary skills? You can pay attention to two appropriate maxims, and you can let the students enjoy literature as simply and as happily as you should let them talk.

First Maxim   "You can lead a horse to water, buy you can't make him drink." If he really wants to drink, you can't stop him either. You can't make the nonreader read, but if he really wants to—if he is thirsty for reading—you can't make him stop. There are many specific ways to make uninvolved students thirsty for books.

Provide some salt. "Salt" the school with attractive, colorful books of all kinds. Every school lobby should have frequently changed book displays, especially in bookless communities. All corridors in these schools should have cases of beautifully, invitingly displayed books. Tables and chairs could be placed at intervals in the halls so students will want to sit and look at the books—perhaps even read them. Newspapers and magazines should be available also. And students should be free to talk about what they are reading.

Listening posts should be provided, since so many books now have accompanying records or tapes. Students who do not read well can listen, or listen and read. Where records are not available, tapes can be made by teachers or other good readers—including students—and used for favorite stories and other readings. If a public address system is available, there can be a story or book of the week partly read or told, the remainder to be read by pupils and discussed in classes.

How can the lobbies and corridors be manned when teachers are so busy? Parents and older boys and girls can do this. In many areas community aides are being hired for hall duty. They can also be trained to read aloud to younger pupils. Reading is catching, and when the older "horses" begin reading, the colts and yearlings will surely follow.

We can encourage the community—the general public—to involve students in literary experiences. The general public can help students read. Books must move out of the schools and into the world in which students live. Why not books in buses and on trains, books in all waiting rooms and stations, books wherever students must go regularly? I mean hospital waiting rooms, doctors' and dentists' offices, shoe stores, and everywhere people gather to wait or to chat. Every Christmas, most stores have a Santa Claus who gives little books to small children. Why confine this to Christmas? Grocery stores would have less trouble with students if they put in reading corners, with appropriate books. In areas where there are few books and few jobs, it would pay stores to hire high school students to read aloud to younger children in such reading corners. There might even be listening posts established here like those suggested for schools.

Public service organizations, such as the police department, the fire department, should prepare books for students. If youngsters like Santa Claus and read the books he gives them, surely they will read books supplied by community agencies. "Officer Friendly" programs in some large cities provide books for young children. These programs should be expanded to cover other areas and older students.

The library is, of course, an important place for books. Like the reservoir that contains a lot of good, fresh water, the library has a great many excellent books. But a horse might find it difficult to drink from a reservoir because of the high fence surrounding it. The uninvolved nonreader can sometimes find the library a cold and threatening place, with a "high fence" of many rules surrounding the books.

I am not criticizing all public and school libraries. Many are warm, friendly, colorful, inviting places where students are led to books and encouraged to read. Unfortunately, some are pretty forbidding, with books bound in dull colors, fines imposed for late return, limited selections, and an air of deadly quiet. This may not be too bad for those students who have access to books at home or elsewhere, but it is wrong for those who have no other way to get at books. If they are defeated or turned away here for any reason, they may turn against books forever.

Libraries for nonreaders must be warm, inviting places with many books on all levels. Public and school libraries should not always separate children's books from others, because poor readers who are maturing will *not* go to children's rooms to read the only books they can manage. It is impossible, in these areas, to adhere to the usual library lists because many books that are right for adults and adolescents do not appear on these lists. These are books of high interest but low reading level. Some are controversial, but they will be read if they are made available. I have seen normally uninvolved children, adolescents, and adults go into the Drum and Spear Book Store at 14th and Euclid Streets in Washington, D.C. You may have heard of this trouble-torn area. There has been disorder: a woman was shot by a policeman, stores have been burned, and windows broken—but the Drum and Spear remains untouched, and a constant stream of people go in to read and buy books.

Possibly not all books in a library are suitable for all students, but *there must be no censorship*. In fact, censorship is impossible, and we only fool ourselves if we think that there is any book students cannot get hold of. Let the students read, and know the books they are reading. Then discuss them openly and suggest others. Demand no book reports; demand no participation; nothing—just fill the rooms and halls and libraries and stores with books that they want to read, and let them go!

If they have difficulty, if you notice that students listen but do not read well, you can begin to teach reading skills in the upper-elementary and secondary grades and with adult students. Reading skills must be taught with total immersion through the early years.[2] But even young children should not be limited to initial and final sounds or to a lockstep reading program. They too must be so surrounded by books, so regularly read to, so often given books that they see reading as a simple and expected accomplishment like talking. Everybody *talks;* everybody *reads!*

Second Maxim   "You can catch more flies with honey than with vinegar." Too many people make reading a nasty dose of medicine. They correct too much in the early years, separate the poor readers and brand them incompetent, mistake too many speech differences for reading difficulties, assign too many dull readers, and make reading a chore instead of a joy. This is wrong even where sensitive parents and alert librarians or others can repair the damage; it is fatal where there is no person to come to the aid of the helpless student.

One of our minority cultures introduces books to babies in a marvelous way. Before each child can walk or talk, they give him his first book with a bit of honey inside. The child—who explores nearly everything with his tongue tastes this. Who are we to say that he does not fall in love with books forever the moment he tastes that honey? Forever, he associates sweetness with books. And that is what we want, isn't it?

How can this be done? Failure must never be associated with reading where there is a possibility that youngsters may someday dislike reading.

If, for reading skills, groups must be formed according to levels, there must be other reading groups based on interests. Books and journals should be written by students and read by them to other students and to adults. Learning styles should be studied carefully and students permitted to use whatever style best helps them learn—programmed, linguistic, kinesthetic, language experience, phonic, basal reader, or whatever. Most of these students should not be given the usual tests, since tests are terrible experiences for many and mean little with this group, anyway. Teachers, older students, and anybody else who will should read aloud to students. Parts of stories can be read and students encouraged to find out how the story ends. If they won't—or can't—the endings should be read to them. They should listen to recorded stories.

Students should be encouraged to make their own books. They should illustrate these books, and *no* critical remarks should be made about them.

Reading incentive seminars should be available on every level in every school. Here, students can be grouped by interest, or heterogeneously. They should have access to many books, especially the easily handled paperbacks. They can read, discuss, role-play, and write (sometimes) about the books; they should be encouraged to read as many as they want.

---

[2] Or perhaps they should *not* be taught. See John Holt's comments about reading in *The Underachieving School* (New York: Pitman Publishing Corp., 1969).

The usual large, indigestible textbooks should be avoided for students who have a tendency to dislike reading. Aim for small, colorful paperback texts for all subjects. In many instances, lessons can be taped so students can listen and read.

Many opportunities should be offered for oral interpretation, usually of short selections. This oral reading should never be done without careful preparation, and no student should be forced to do this against his will. All efforts should be praised.

Instead of the routine comprehension checks, creative ways of evaluating understanding should be developed. For example:

Students can be asked to role-play scenes from stories. They can do this if they have read carefully, and their classmates can check the accuracy of their portrayals.

Slips of paper with correct and incorrect statements can be passed, and students asked to find out whether they are true. They must read to do this.

Individuals or small groups can be assigned certain information to find. Here heterogeneity is important.

Obviously, reading must be made enjoyable or it simply will not be done. Vinegar will catch no flies. Unhappy experiences with reading will produce no eager readers.

We often talk about the dreadful failures of students—their stupidity, their inability to learn to read; but perhaps we should take a look at our failures.

Have we tried to lead a student to the trough of learning and forced his head into a book? And have we then fumed and fussed because he will not read?

Have we kept books away from students because we don't want to confuse them with books until they know letters and sounds? Have we then tested and corrected and sighed because they dislike reading tests, and books?

Surround students with beautiful, meaningful, involving books! Surround students with books they have written. Let them listen to stories and books read by others. Insist that books become an important and exciting part of the environment! Lead them to books and make books sweet for them. Then let students read! If we can do this, we won't be able to stop them.

Or try a "sustained silent reading" program as advocated by Lyman Hunt and others. At a designated period in the school day *everyone* reads—students, teachers, principal.

Some Specifics

"I have a name," says this student as he rejects the labels reserved for him. He is not simply "the slow reader," "the deprived child," "the disadvantaged Chicano," "one of the rural poor," "the immigrant," "the urban immigrant," "the black." He may belong in one or more of these categories, but he is primarily himself—a person who is uninvolved in the reading process and alienated by the usual methods used to reclaim him. He *has* a name, and the teacher who hopes to reclaim him must learn what it is and how to use it to advantage.

The reader may see himself in photographs like those from *The Family of Man.* When these photographs were passed out in a junior high school classroom in a large city several years ago, there was silence in the room as students looked in wonder at faces like their own and faces different from theirs. They looked at people living many different life styles in many different lands but all alike in a family feeling—in a love of each other, of home, and of family ties. After several lessons with these photographs, the students wanted to keep them. They asked why no teacher had used them before. They wanted to use them not just in English but in history and in science and in physical education classes. They read the faces in the photographs; then they read the captions. Then, having succeeded and being encouraged by success, they were willing to try to read a book.

Alienated readers in junior high school who rejected the usual remedial reading—characterized by endless practice in phonics, the use of elementary school materials, and the assumption by the teacher that incapacity caused poor reading—were able to read when photographs were used to "hook" them, to show them themselves, and to begin to interest them in important things that can be found in books. Photographs, then, have impact and must be used.

> Often the faces speak what words can never say. People! flung wide and far, born into toil, struggle, blood, and dreams. To the question, "What will the story be of The Family of Man across the near or far future?" some would reply, "For the answers, read if you can the strange and baffling eyes of youth." [3]

The teacher who understands that alienation from reading is not necessarily based on inability but just as frequently on the pupil's agony at years of being unseen as himself—years of trying to say who he is and being ignored, years of being classified by those who think they know him—will start with whatever material says to the pupil "I know you; I know who you are; I know your name." Photographs can help do this.

Reading with Relevance

Today's adolescent may have tuned out the written word—even the spoken word—but he has not tuned out all sound. Music can reach him. It has impact and can be used to involve the alienated reader.

In a big city, a group of fifth and sixth grade boys sat in a special reading

---

[3] From E. Steichen, ed., *The Family of Man* (New York: Simon & Schuster, 1955).

group, supposedly because they could not read. The reading specialist worked with them regularly and desperately in an effort to get them ready for junior high school. In this city, students go to junior high school when they have reached the age of 13 years and 7 months. Ready or not—nonreader, first, second, sixth, or ninth grade level—they go. These boys were on just about every reading level, according to their tests. Then, one spring morning they were introduced to a colorful, small, but grown-up looking book. Racing cars not bunnies! A black leopard, not a cuddly pussy cat! Photographs of boys growing up to do exciting things, not Dick and Jane waiting for Daddy! Music with words that can be used for structural analysis, "Call Me Irresponsible," for example: *ir*respons*ible*, *un*reli*able*, *un*deni*able.* Or "The Impossible Dream." And stories about real people who do brave things.

I visited the class one day when these boys—the poor readers, the alienated, disadvantaged, uninterested boys, the potential dropouts—were reading a rather long selection from Frank Bonham's *Durango Street.* The teacher read aloud while the boys followed silently; they read aloud some; and they discussed the action. Quite obviously they were involved—reading, understanding, and enjoying. On another day I saw them read Richard Wright's "The Flight," finish it, and discuss it during one class period. A boy sent on an errand by the principal returned, picked up the book, sat beside me, and read silently to catch up. I was prepared to help, but he didn't need me. He joined the discussion.

The teacher and I asked the boys why they suddenly began to read so well. We taped their answers. "These stories are interesting, and they are about us. We don't like baby books and stuff for little kids. We like fights and adventure." And, believe me, they do!

Imaginative Reading

It is absolutely necessary for the teacher to use the right materials, not to limit reluctant readers to poorly written, carelessly illustrated, patronizing little stories. Their world should be a point of departure for alienated readers. From it they can be led into the world of the imagination.

Role-playing is an important way to involve the alienated and to tune them in to reading. Preceded by some simple theater games, role-playing is not just play acting but a combination of language arts skills allied with the less tangible understanding and interpreting skills. The nonverbal person who acts out with rude gestures and fighting might well be the one who can improve his reading through role-playing. The one who needs to be active once in a while can *be* active—constructively—here.

I have spoken about recognizing the errors of the past in attempting to reclaim the alienated reader. Two major variables are the attitude and the expectation of the teacher. The attitude must be positive, and there must be expectation of success. This sounds simple, but it isn't. Students who have met only failure in school expect to be expected to fail, and the face of the teacher on the first day can simply reinforce this. But that isn't all. Immature and colorless materials reveal all a pupil needs to know about the attitude and expectation of his teacher. Books that are too big and threatening can induce failure also.

What are some characteristics of a good reading and literature program?

The books are colorful, mature, and small enough to be easily handled.

Photographs and reproductions of painting and sculpture are carefully selected for appeal, relevance, and beauty.

Headlines lead pupils into the story. (These help with the reading skills of skimming, scanning, and getting the main idea also.)

Short quotations, poems, and short, short stories like "Cemetery Path" and "Dinner Party" are full of excitement but are easily read.

Carefully selected paperback libraries extend the reading into other books and, hopefully, will "hook" pupils on reading more and more.

Records with the beginnings of stories and with poems and songs are useful. All teachers cannot read or sing well. (The *listen and read* technique can be used here.)

Manuals for use with your class' books may give you other ideas and suggestions on new, unusual ways to approach whatever you're studying.

Review of the Specifics

How, then, does a teacher—or any interested person—reclaim the alienated reader?

He approaches him in a human and accepting way, expecting him to succeed. He makes an effort to "speak" to him.

He provides a program that will involve him in every way—his feelings, his sense of himself, the senses of hearing, seeing, and touching. Pictures—black and white and in color—show his world and add other new and exciting worlds. Short selections are heard or read successfully. New methods like role-playing are used as comprehension checks.

He stimulates discussion with music, poetry, pictures, and relevant reading materials.

He fills the environment with new, small, manageable books; with materials that "hook" the uninvolved student on reading. Then he keeps him on the hook.

The alienated reader must be reclaimed. Reach out to him, touch his world, accept him, expect much of him, respect him, use the resources within him, learn from him what he is, open the world to him; understand that reading involves more than the printed word.

If nothing works, you will at least have tried. So be creative; try again.

Strategies to Help Learners Mesh
Literature and Reading

One day I visited an inner-city high school in which a special, last-ditch class had been made up of tenth grade boys who were failing in every subject —or in nearly every subject. They were perfunctory readers and seldom, if ever, took books home to study. A teacher asked for a chance to experiment with them, and when I visited the class I found them seated in a circle discussing—arguing about—Sillitoe's "Loneliness of the Long-Distance Runner." It was obvious from the discussion that, despite the British setting, these alienated American boys fully understood the situation of the disadvantaged English lad. They even understood what he was really saying about reading in one passage in which he discusses his governor at Borstal for whom he intends to write his experiences. This man, the runner says, will fail to comprehend the story that he reads. Not only were the boys taking Borstal and the governor in stride, they were understanding exactly what was being said in this and in other passages.

Another boy borrowed Hawthorne's *The Scarlet Letter* from a collection, to the great surprise of his English teacher. "Do you know what that book is about, and that it is hard to read?" asked the teacher. "Ain't it about a bad woman?" (a euphemism) the boy asked. When the answer was in the affirmative, he took it for the weekend and returned with several pages covered with words and their definitions. Since he was unable to understand the story because he did not know the words, he had labored diligently to find the meanings in a dictionary. He discussed the story with his teacher and began to understand the theme and content of the novel. When he finished the story, he said to his teacher, "She wasn't really a bad woman, was she?" (Neil Postman tells this story.)

In a New Jersey classroom, I watched a class read a poem and discuss the meaning of each line. The poem was Theodore Roethke's "My Papa's Waltz." Students discussed the poem, line by line, and rejected old interpretations as new lines were placed on the board and the meaning became clear. (Dr. Postman taught this lesson.)

My Papa's Waltz [4]

The Whiskey on your breath
Could make a small boy dizzy
But I held on like death
Such waltzing was not easy.

We romped until the pans
Slid from the Kitchen shelf;

---

[4] Theodore Roethke, "My Papa's Waltz," copyright 1942 by Hearst Magazine Inc. From *Collected Poems of Theodore Roethke* (Garden City, N.Y.: Doubleday & Co., 1966), p. 45. Reprinted by permission of Doubleday & Company, Inc.

My mother's countenance
Could not unfrown itself.

The hand that held my wrist
Was battered on one knuckle;
At every step I missed
My right ear scraped a buckle.

You beat time on my head
With a palm caked hard by dirt,
Then waltzed me off to bed
Still clinging to your shirt.

Let me tell you about Al. He was sitting at the back of the room at first, as sullen and uninterested as usual. At the interpretation of the first line he looked disgusted, by the third he was impatient, and when the entire poem was on the chalkboard he came suddenly and loudly to life, for the first time that term. "Aw, let me tell you what that's all about," he said. And he did. The poem was relevant and meaningful for him.

There are other poems like this. Try a unit on war poetry, using Reed's "Naming of Parts," something by Wilfred Owen or Siegfried Sassoon, and perhaps Yeats' "An Irish Airman Foresees His Death." And there are contemporary poets whose works can be used here, too.

Lessons in Meshing Literature and Reading

In addition to the suggestions already made in this chapter, here are several other examples.

The Odyssey is a great classic and a marvelous monster story. Originally it was not read, but told. In one classroom, students listened to the story over a period of several weeks while they created the ancient Greek world out of salt colored with vegetable dyes. Then, as they listened, they made the monsters from wood, soap, clay, or whatever they wanted to use and put them in the correct places on the "salt table" (a large table in the classroom). These students were boys majoring in shop subjects, and had heretofore unscrewed desks, thrown paper, and shown a general disinclination to read or to enjoy literature. In this unit, both ears and fingers were employed and were used for learning. Later, they read some parts of *The Odyssey* and some history and geography to confirm the accuracy of their Greek world, their monsters, and the probable route of Odysseus and his men.

Teachers and students have listened to Alex Haley, coauthor of *The Autobiography of Malcolm X*, tell the story of the years of research he devoted to his new book, *Before this Anger*, in which he traces his family history to its African origin. Students have said that they wanted to do similar research after hearing him. I am convinced that no student will fail to read *Before this Anger;* I know most have already read *The Autobiography of Malcolm X.* The following suggested plan is only one of several which might be tried.[5]

English Curriculum—Neglected Literature—Biography

The Autobiography of Malcolm X
Alex Haley and Malcolm X

Introduction

The Autobiography of Malcolm X has become a classic of American literature. It is the story of one of the assassinated black leaders of America. It is the story of self-realization and challenge. It is the story of the true essence of the problems of black versus white America. It is blunt and pulls no punches on its reader. For the high school students of the District it aids in erasing the image of the glory of the underworld and places in motion the wheels of improving one's status regardless of one's present station. John Hersey, author of such American classics as *A Bell for Adano* and *Hiroshima,* says in the introduction to his new book, *The Algiers Motel Incident,* "I was immeasurably aided in the ventilation of my mind by that surpassingly remarkable document of our time, *The Autobiography of Malcolm X,* which every white American with any pretensions to racial understanding simply must read. I had, besides, over the years, made it my business and pleasure—sometimes—to read the works by Ellison, Richard Wright, James Baldwin, John Kelley, Eldridge Cleaver, and other authors of their race, and I had found, indeed, that life imitated their art, when they achieved it, and that they had prepared me for my work." To support further the importance of this work, it is noteworthy to mention that the 1968 General Electric College Bowl reading list, prepared by Dartmouth College, lists this vital work as one of its major "Books Worth Rereading." Approaches to this work in the classroom vary with the class level.

Questions

1. List and discuss any two major events in the first half of this book which you feel caused Malcolm Little to hate whites and convert to the Black Muslim movement.

2. What characteristics of Malcolm's personality made him a great Muslim minister?

3. Why was he so successful in delivering his message to audiences?

---

[5] From An Experimental Curriculum Resource Bulletin for Secondary Schools: *Neglected Literature* (Washington, D.C.: Department of English, n.d.). Curriculum chairman: Mrs. Rosemary C. Wilson. Curriculum writers: Lovelle W. Golden, Beverly H. Hyman, Lloyd D. Mayfield.

4.   Why did Malcolm leave the Black Muslim organization?

5.   What were some of the results of his break with this group?

6.   According to this book, do the Black Muslims appear to be more religious than political in philosophy? Discuss.

7.   What is the name of the organization which Malcolm founded when he left the Black Muslims? What were the objectives of this organization?

8.   Do you see any connection between the assassination of Malcolm X and the assassinations of other notable black leaders such as Medgar Evers and Martin Luther King, Jr.? Defend your position.

9.   For several years after his assassination, Malcolm X was considered a radical in the civil rights movement. Can you account for the recent change in attitude concerning him among the black leaders of America?

10.   According to the epilog of this work, what is Ossie Davis' opinion of Malcolm X? What major points does he bring out?

11.   Is the epilog necessary to this book? Discuss.

Activities

1.   Have students write comments on each chapter of the book. Give the students the freedom to react to one another's points of view.

2.   Write compositions on the various personality traits which made Malcolm X a leader.

3.   Prepare a panel discussion on the topic "Assassinated Black Leaders."

Alternate Biographies of Negroes

Marian Anderson, *My Lord, What a Morning*

Lerone Bennett, Jr., *What Manner of Man: A Biography of Martin Luther King, Jr., 1929–1968*

Earl Conrad, *Harriet Tubman*

Sammy Davis, Jr., *Yes, I Can*

Phillip S. Foner, *Frederick Douglass: A Biography*

Althea Gibson with Ed Fitzgerald, *I Always Wanted to Be Somebody*

James J. Greene, *Wendell Phillips: A Biography*

W. C. Handy, *Father of the Blues*

Ann Moody, *Coming of Age in Mississippi*

Hugh Mulzac (Capt.), *A Star to Steer By*

LeRoy (Satchel) Paige, *Maybe I'll Pitch Forever*

Gordon Parks, *A Choice of Weapons*

Sidney Poitier, *The Long Journey*

Bill Russell, *Go Up for Glory*

Madeline R. Stratton, *Negroes Who Helped Build America*

Ethel Waters, *His Eye Is on the Sparrow*

Finally, if your students really are "unhooked," secure a number of short, fascinating books (even comic books) and find a page full of exciting but unfinished happenings. Or perhaps you prefer gripping, funny, or mysterious events. Make sure that the events are not explained on the back of the page.

Now put a page from each book on the desks of your students, one page per student. (For this lesson, it is best to wait until you know the students pretty well, including their interests and reading levels). Sometimes a picture with just an intriguing caption is what you need.

Ask students to discuss in small groups, one to one, or with the whole class what they *think* they have. Then put it into context by providing a part—or all—of the rest. Later, students may devise lessons like this.

Instead of using different works, you may want to use parts of one work in this way. Such books as *The Outsiders, Durango Street, The Cool World, Two Blocks Apart,* and *The Civil War as They Knew It* are useful. You can find others.

Use poems in the same way, placing lines from the poem (interspersed with appropriate illustrations) on students' desks. In the final chapter of this book is a lesson on Langston Hughes' "I, Too, Sing America." This, as well as some poems mentioned in Chapter 5, can be used effectively in this way.

The manuals for new literature and language arts series such as *Gateway Impact, Crossroads, Voices of Man* will also help you mesh literature with reading.

7

Cardozo High School, an inner-city school in Washington, D.C., often tries innovative ideas. A Washington newspaper published this article written by Gregory Adams, which was first seen in *Just Rappin'*, a collection of writings by Cardozo students in 1968. In 1969 the book was published in another form: a kit of materials called *Cardozo Raps*.

Man's Inhumanity to Man [1]
Gregory Reginald Adams

man (man) n. (men) 1. A human being, esp. a mature male human being. 2. The human race, mankind.

inhuman (in-hū'-man) adj. Lacking the good qualities of mankind; cruel. Syn. brutal, savage, barbarous, ruthless, merciless, ferocious.

Washington, D.C. 1. Capitol of the United States of America. 2. Large Afro-American ghetto. 3. Breeding place of the brutal, savage, barbarous, ruthless, merciless, ferocious man.

The words you have just read describe the world I live in, the world we all live in. It is a world of startling realizations, realizations which we all have to face at some point in our life. Was man meant to be the vicious animal which he is, or does he wish to be that way? Is he capable of changing the future he is heading for, or is he doomed to meet such a destiny? What makes my world the way it is? All of these things I shall discuss in this writing.

My world is D.C.; it always has been and will be. I will die either trying to better it or falling into its vices. Right now, my world is a bad one, so not too long ago I decided to find out why.

It was on a Saturday night, and seeing as how it was February, it was snowing. I put on my coat, picked up my pencil and pad, and went out the door. While crossing the street on my way to the bus stop, I noticed a cat smashed in the street. I remember wondering whether the killer did it intentionally or not. I caught the bus and rode down to Fourteenth and T Streets. I knew it was foolish,

---

[1] Gregory Reginald Adams, "Man's Inhumanity to Man," in *Cardozo Raps*, Washington, D.C., 1969. Reprinted by permission of the author.

but I intended to interview some people. I imagined how they would look at me after I told them I would like to have their views on "Man's Inhumanity to Man" for a high school English paper.

I spotted one cat; he looked at me, I looked at him. He looked at me, and I looked at him. It was obvious what he was. Everything about him was so cool: his clothes, the way he walked and talked, the manner in which he carried himself. He was a pusher (and probably a lot of other things on the side). When I asked him his views on "Man's Inhumanity to Man," he lashed right into me. "Big time school-boy, huh? Mr. Joe College. No sir. You ain't gonna mess with no jive man. What you doin' talkin' to me? Ain't you scared I might try to pop you with a needle right here on the street?" I had to play it cool to let this dude know that he wasn't shaking me up. "Be cool man. I just want you to answer the question," I said. He just looked at me for a second, then: "Look man, this is my job. You gotta write that paper so you can get out of high school, then into college, then out to get you a good job. Well, if that's what you want, okay. I tried that once, but it wasn't my thing. This is. If people is stupid enough to get messed up with the stuff, well that's too bad."

One more person to interview and I was ready to go home. I spotted a woman coming out of the Safeway struggling with three large bags of groceries. "Need any help, miss?" I asked. "Where's your wagon?" she replied. I explained to her that I was not a carrier boy and that I was interviewing people on the street for an English paper. I think she was a little suspicious at first, but she agreed to answer my question while we walked to her house. I was impressed with what she said. "You know something? I feel like the only thing that's been inhuman to me is this damn city's government. Let me tell you. A few years ago, maybe before you were even born, I used to live in Southeast. Southeast was nothin' to brag about in those days. I wasn't exactly satisfied with the house me and my kids were livin' in, my husband's God knows where, but at least it was ours. Then this city got the bright idea to rebuild out there. They said they was going to build low-income housing projects and when they was through we could live in them. Well, practically everybody had to move to some other part of the city and we was lucky to get the rat hole we livin' in now." We turned down Eighteenth Street. "They built all those town houses and luxury apartments out there for them rich folks and the ones who was livin' out there at first can't afford to go back. They did build a few projects out there, but they got a waiting list a mile long. It's a damn shame." She stopped in the middle of the block. "Well, here it is." It was a basement apartment, typical of the kind of homes Southeast refugees live in now. From the outside it looked just like she described it, a rat hole. She turned and yelled into a broken windowpane. "Jaimie, come out here and help me with these bags." She turned back to me. "What do I owe you?" "Nothing," I said. She didn't try to argue.

Gregory talked with and wrote about other people that night: an unmarried mother on relief, a prostitute, a friend who dressed well and drove a big car. He said about that friend:

What is he? I think Bay is a product of this city. Somewhere along the line, Bay was probably forced by the city to move into a cheap rat hole somewhere, living with a mother who probably didn't want him.

The article ends this way:

> I wonder how drunks had gotten to him and told him who to be inhuman to? How old was Bay when dope was pushed on him and he was forced to turn to crime to support his habit? Like so many other people, Bay had to make up his mind to fight hard in this city or let it kill him.
>
> And what about our city government? Can it be helped, or must it go on being an instrument of death? All of these questions and problems could be solved if people lived by one word:
>
> *humanity* (hū-man'-i-ti) n.   1. mankind.   2. The qualities of kindness and sympathy.   3. Quality of being human.

In Greenville, Mississippi, the students often begin the term worn out; they have spent the summer working with cotton in the flat delta region surrounding the city. I worked with three classes there, and we faced the question of humanity that Gregory had. Another Gregory had faced it, too—Dick Gregory. I read part of his autobiography to my classes in Greenville.

> Momma had to take us to Homer G. Phillips, the free hospital, the city hospital for Negroes. We'd stand in line and wait for hours, smiling and Uncle Tomming every time a doctor or a nurse passed by. We'd feel good when one of them smiled back and didn't look at us as though we were dirty and had no right coming down there. All the doctors and nurses at Homer G. Phillips were Negro, too.
>
> I remember one time when a doctor in white walked up and said, "What's wrong with him?" as if he didn't believe that anything was.
>
> Momma looked at me and looked at him and shook her head. "I sure don't know, Doctor, but he cried all night long. Held his stomach."
>
> "Bring him in and get his clothes off."
>
> I was so mad the way he was talking to my Momma that I bit down too hard on the thermometer. It broke in my mouth. The doctor slapped me across my face.
>
> "Both of you go stand in the back of the line and wait your turn."
>
> My Momma had to say "I'm sorry, Doctor" and go to the back of the line. She had five other kids at home, and she never knew when she'd have to bring another down to the City Hospital.[2]

I wrote the word "human" on the board, then placed "in" before it and "ity" after it. The word was not discussed at this point, but we did talk about the feelings Dick, his mother, and the others must have had, and about our own feelings about the doctor.

We went then to a part of John Steinbeck's *The Pearl.* The baby, Coyotito, has been bitten by a scorpion, and his parents, the Indian couple Juana and Kino, take him to a doctor.

---

[2] From the book *Nigger: An Autobiography* by Dick Gregory with Robert Lipsyte. Copyright © 1964 by Dick Gregory Enterprises, Inc. Published by E. P. Dutton & Co., Inc. and used with their permission.

The servant from the gate came to the open door and stood waiting to be noticed.
"Yes?" the doctor asked.
"It is a little Indian with a baby. He says a scorpion stung it."
The doctor put his cup down gently before he let his anger rise.
"Have I nothing better to do than cure insect bites for 'little Indians'? I am a doctor, not a veterinary."
"Yes, Patron," said the servant.
"Has he any money?" the doctor demanded. "No, they never have any money. I, I alone in the world am supposed to work for nothing, and I am tired of it. See if he has any money."
At the gate the servant opened the door a little and looked at the waiting people.
"Have you money to pay for the treatment?"
Now Kino reached into a secret place somewhere under his blanket. He brought out a paper folded many times. He unfolded it, until at last there came to view eight small seed pearls, as ugly and gray as little ulcers, almost valueless. The servant took the paper and closed the gate again, but this time he was not gone long. He opened the gate just wide enough to pass the paper back.
"The doctor has gone out," he said. "He was called to a case." And he shut the gate quickly out of shame.
For a long time Kino stood in front of the gate with Juana beside him. Slowly he put his hat on his head. Then, without waning, he struck the gate a crushing blow with his fist. He looked down in wonder at his split knuckles and at the blood that flowed down between his fingers.[3]

Then came the questions:
What is a human being, and how should human beings be treated?
What is inhumanity? (Here, touch lightly on a structural analysis of the word "inhumanity," using the chalkboard or an overhead projector. The words "human," "humane," and "inhuman" can be developed with or without a dictionary.)
How were the two doctors alike? How different?
Did the doctors see Dick's family and Coyotito's as human? Find specific examples to support your answer.
Have you ever experienced anything like this, or do you know of anyone who has?
Have you read stories about inhumanity in newspapers, magazines, or books?

Relevance and the Humanities

When we begin work in the humanities, we should have a great deal of illustrative material in the room. Since our students may be interested in

---

[3] John Steinbeck, *The Pearl* (New York: Viking Press, 1947). Copyright 1945 by John Steinbeck. Reprinted by permission of The Viking Press, Inc. Also in Charlotte K. Brooks and L. Trout, eds., *I've Got a Name* (New York: Holt, Rinehart and Winston, 1968), pp. 54–55; this is level 1 of the *Impact* series, a collection of books designed for alienated or uninvolved secondary school students.

abstract ideas, concrete examples must be available. Records like "Ode to Billy Joe" or other ballads about man's inhumanity or his humanity will make the idea of a study of the humanities real for uninvolved students. Current newspaper articles or editorials like this one can be posted or copied—at least in part—for study.

My Lai, Justice, and Military Realities [4]

"And they utterly destroyed all that was in the city, both man and woman, young and old."

Now Joshua was not indicted under Article 118 of the Uniform Code of Military Justice for the slaughter of the civilian population of Jericho. But then "the Lord was with Joshua," we are told. First Lieutenant William Laws Calley, Jr., may not have been so fortunate in his companions, spiritual or temporal, at My Lai.

We do not know what happened that balmy March morning of last year when Charlie Company of the American Division's 11th Infantry Brigade stormed into the hamlet. It may never be entirely clear what took place or why it happened. The "truth" of that bloody day lies in the eyes of many beholders, blurred by the scar-tissue of time.

That deep sense of horror stems fundamentally from the illogical but firmly held conviction that clean-cut American boys simply are incapable of such acts. It is an intrinsic component of the American myth that somehow we are different—and hence better—than other people. We can accept the fact that the Germans liquidated six million Jews. We are not surprised to learn that the Russians shot thousands of Polish prisoners in the Katyn forest in 1940. Even the French execution of some 15,000 Moslems during the Algerian war does not trouble us unduly. These are the acts, after all, of old and corrupt cultures.

And yet we recoil with horror at the suggestion that a boy who drank milkshakes and played football could gun down a two-year-old. We do this despite the fact that our intellect tells us that the dark side of his nature, which lurks in every man, is not tamed when he dons his country's uniform. Quite the contrary.

It is possible—and necessary—to try to explain, if not to condone, what appears to have happened at My Lai. The area was called Pinkville for a reason. It was called that because it had been a Viet Cong stronghold for years. It lay within what is known as a "free-fire zone," meaning that everyone within it is assumed to be hostile and hence an appropriate target for bombing and shelling.

Charlie Company was a green, understrength unit which in its month in Vietnam had sustained heavy casualties in the Pinkville area. Its men, according to statements, were expecting strong resistance. At least initially, they appear to have been unaware of and unprepared for the presence of women and children in My Lai.

Viet Cong do not wear brass buttons and chevrons. They wear the same black pajamas as any Vietnamese peasant. Men and women dress alike and tend to be substantially similar in stature. In any event, you are just as dead if shot by a woman—or a child—as you are if a man pulls the trigger.

No nation of its own free will has embraced communism. None has emerged

---

[4] *The Washington Star,* December 7, 1969. Reprinted by permission.

from it. President Thieu's government hardly can be held up as a shining example to civics classes. But in its constitution and because of the reality of American influence, the concept of free choice exists.

Nothing that may have happened at My Lai affects this. If men who were afraid or angry or brimming with bitterness committed atrocities, this does not alter the issues behind the war.

Something more than people died at My Lai. Call it a dream of innocence, an illusion of perfectibility. But those many millions of Americans who have gone out to dark places around the world, done what they had to do, and come home again are unlikely to throw the first stone.

After the My Lai trial we will be the same people we were before it. Evil will remain no more—and no less—than the obverse of good. If there were no Satan, there would be no point in a God. The world will go on. Problems will remain. Men of good will try to solve them.

What can be done with an editorial like this to strengthen a humanities program so it will really involve students?

The article can be read and discussed in terms of the human condition and in terms of what it says about what has happened in the past and what is happening now.

Parts of the article can be taped and played for the class while photographs of the Civil War and more recent wars are viewed, possibly on slides. Great war paintings like Picasso's *Guernica* can be seen and discussed as they relate to what the editorial says about war.

The story of Joshua can be found and read from the Bible, and other specific references in the editorial can be found and discussed by students. For example:

The German liquidation of Jews (*The Diary of Anne Frank,* book and film, can be used in this work).

The Russian killings of Polish prisoners (Kosinski's *The Painted Bird* can also be used effectively).

The French execution of Moslems during the Algerian War (the film *Night and Fog* might be used here).

There are many other photographs, paintings, novels, essays, and many musical selections which can be found to reinforce this introduction to the humanities. Do not neglect the poems of Siegfried Sassoon, Wilfred Owen, Stephen Spender, William Butler Yeats, and contemporary poets who are protesting now against the current war.

A good humanities program involves more than using material written by students, selecting appropriate readings, asking the right questions, and using appropriate and closely related material from literature, social studies, art, and music. The real intent of the humanities is to help students see man's creative drive toward personal and social freedom through the meaning and value he finds in the great ideas of literature, art, and music. There must be a focus on those values that help the student see himself and others as human beings with judgments, concepts, tastes. There must be a blending of aesthetic and intellectual components of the human heritage so that students can see in the present context as well as that of the past those values which make them human. And they must be helped to see that these values will extend into the future, far beyond the experiences of secondary school.

You may have listened to those who say that humanities is for the bright student who reads well and is already committed to in-depth study of those disciplines which comprise the program. You may have heard that only the highly motivated and the splendid reader can possibly understand and become interested in humanities. Quite simply, I disagree. This is my position: if years of dull readers, poorly taught grammar and usage, badly organized literature anthologies, and spelling and punctuation drills have turned them off, there is every chance that they can be turned on again by a strong program in the humanities. If they can first see themselves as human beings and define themselves in terms of humanity—; if they are to hear and see great works in which man is central, with his gropings, his weaknesses, his failures, his greatness—; if they are to see what man has thought about his gods and nature, himself and his own nature—; if they are to share questions about themselves and other human beings—; if they are to see clearly what inhumanity is and has always been—; if they are to relate the past to the present and to the future through appropriate readings, records, films and tapes—; if they are to come to grips with humanness—then they must have a chance to experience the humanities.

Experiencing the Humanities

An exciting humanities course is more important for the uninvolved than for those others who already see where they are as human beings in this world. Although this book is for secondary school students, teaching the humanities should really begin in a preschool program. It should accompany the skills program and should be an integral part of the curriculum from beginning to end. Without it, the skills program is, has always been, and always will be unsuccessful with the student who sees himself as different from—and very early senses himself to be inferior to—the other students. He will respond— body, mind, and soul—to the kinds of experiences he does not ordinarily expect and has not usually had in classrooms where year after year he has been bored, frustrated, and unseen.

I do not propose catering to the whims and fancies of students to try to keep them entertained. I do propose that, after learning their interests, needs, and competences, you design with them a program in the humanities that will open them to themselves and to the world of man—that will bring the whole world of man to them.

Help them explore the thought and feelings of man in their search for identity, meaning, and direction—in their desire to know "Who am I?" "Why am I here?" "Where am I going?"

Help them to discover what man has felt, thought, believed, and done as he has lived through the ages, expressing his attitudes toward himself, mankind, and the universe; as he has looked for meaning and for freedom.

Help them to see how various fields of study are not discrete but are connected: art, music, literature, drama, history, perhaps even philosophy.

Help them find adventure in experiencing these discoveries with joy.

And start, perhaps, with this instead of with any of the other ways of helping students learn English.

Why? Because there are many ways to discover yourself as your students discover themselves in the humanities; despite language and cultural differences, they will respond with you to the beauty, to the emotional and intellectual appeal of what you share.

The practical assumption is that you are going to work with your students alone, although the work is better if you can learn with art, music, and social studies teachers. Most new teachers everywhere must work pretty much alone unless they are in special internships. I will assume, too, that you are teaching a heterogeneous group of students who read on different levels, have varying likes and dislikes about music and art, and have little opportunity for imaginative and creative expression.

A short film like *Clay, Glass, The Red Balloon,* or *The Leaf* is a good way to begin. Or a reproduction of *Guernica* on the wall while the record player or tape recorder plays warlike selections.

You might choose to have photographs from *The Family of Man* displayed around the room; as the class enters, the rather sentimental "Scarlet Ribbons" or some more sophisticated piece of music with a family theme can be played.

Perhaps you can begin with a contemporary work like Warren Miller's *The Cool World* and move backward or horizontally in time to find and explore similar themes in novels, short stories, art, music.

Or you can use an older work like *Romeo and Juliet* and pair it with *West Side Story.* Compare the opera and the ballet, the play and the film to help students see the theme and themselves in different ways.

Poetry like "Ithaka" by Cavafy can be studied; students may read Tennyson's "Ulysses" and the odysseys of many other men. *Huckleberry Finn,* a kind of odyssey, may well fit in here.

In any of these experiences, the students must see themselves if they are to understand the work. Black poetry, Spanish flamenco music, and African works may be useful. Contemporary music and films will help to do this.

A Sample Unit

A group of teachers in the Washington, D.C., Public Schools prepared a humanities program. One unit should be enough to illustrate what can be done for students by a group committed to humanities for all students.[5]

The following questions are abstracted from the book *Teaching as a Subversive Activity* by Neil Postman and Charles Weingartner. Some or all of them might profitably be used by the humanities teacher in this unit in two ways. First, they might be given to the students to spark their thinking and feeling about themselves and who they are. One or two might later be applied to the work of literature, art, or music being studied, thereby inviting comparisons and the awareness of different attitudes about these "universal" value indicators. For instance, question 3 might be aptly applied to John, the adolescent hero of *Go Tell It on the Mountain* since he is trying to better understand himself by understanding the adults who have helped to shape his life.

1. What do you worry about? What seem to be the causes of these worries? Could you eliminate any of these worries? How? Which of these worries do you think are shared by other people?

2. What important ideas do you have that you would like to share? How would you go about letting others know about them?

3. How would you like to be similar to and different from the adults you now know when you become an adult?

4. What, if anything, is worth dying for? How did you come to believe this?

5. What, if anything, is worth living for? How did you come to believe this?

6. How can you tell the bad guys from the good guys? How can you distinguish good from evil?

7. When you hear, observe, read, how do you know what it means? Where does meaning come from? What does meaning mean?

8. What do you consider man's most important ideas? Where did they come from? Why?

9. Which of man's ideas do you feel we'd be better off forgetting? How did you decide?

10. What is worth knowing? How did you decide? What are some ways to go about knowing what is worth knowing?

Unit I   Search for Self in Four Significant Periods of Time Modern Period: late nineteenth century to mid-1950s

General Concepts

Realism expressed in the rejection of middle-class ideals of morality or respectability.

---

[5] This unit, called "The Search for Self," is taken from "Humanities, a Pilot Twelfth Grade program for Public Senior High Schools in Washington, D.C." (Washington, D.C.: Humanities in the Curriculum Department and the Department of English, 1969–1970), unpublished. Chairman: Mrs. Jessie M. Wright, Leon Berkowitz, Charlotte Bostick, Patricia Hoffman. Consultant: Elva Wells.

Concern expressed for the individualistic in character—the eccentric, impassioned, or sensitive character.

Interest in the vernacular displayed.

Naturalism, an expansion of realism, gave expression of interest in the conflict of social forces and concern for the less pleasant aspects of life. A great deal of sympathy is shown for the proletariat.

Some concepts and developments which have influenced the contemporary temper are:

Revolt against reason
Superiority of one's conscience
Social Darwinism
Henry James' Pragmatism
Carl Jung's "collective unconscious"
Albert Einstein's theory of relativity
Freudian psychology
Materialism
Influence of Nietzsche
Technology and the emergence of "mass-man"
Influence of Marxism
Pessimism, disillusionment, skepticism, personal insecurity
Man's inhumanity to man: World War II, concentration camps, massacres, atomic bombs
Nationalistic feelings in Africa and Asia
Recognition of cultural achievements of the non-Western world

Music: Jazz

The medium of jazz represents a search for the black man's identity because for so long it was the only means of self-expression open to him. It was often easier for a black man to become a jazz musician than an elevator operator, which offers decidedly less in the way of artistic possibilities.

Jazz, then, must be a highly important art form to contain the aspirations, despair, and the entire general history of a people in America. This once-neglected subculture has, in recent years, become a fully recognized art form, and it is now agreed that it is America's only indigenous music.

List of Compositions and Albums:

1. Bessie Smith
    Queen of the Blues, Bessie Smith
    The Bessie Smith Story, Columbia 503–05
2. John Coltrane
    Ascension
    Cannonball and Coltrane, Washington, D.C., Public Library RAL 2547
3. Miles Davis
    Miles Ahead, Washington, D.C., Public Library RAL 551
    Porgy and Bess
4. Charlie Parker, *The World of Charlie Parker,* Washington, D.C., Public Library RAL 2338

Because it was a music of ill repute, many jazz artists, in order to make it more palatable to middle-class audiences—who formed the paying public—compromised with a refined, well-honed style. See, for example:

1. Duke Ellington
    Hi Fi Ellington Uptown MUS RAL 1058 (Washington, D.C., Library)

Ellingtonia, Brunswick 58002, 58012
Concert of Sacred Music, Victor LSP 3582
2. Count Basie
   The Best of Count Basie, MUS RAL 484
   The Count, Camden 395
3. Lionel Hampton, *Taste of Hamp,* Glad-Hamp 1009 S
4. Cannonball Adderly, *Quintet in San Francisco,* Riverside 311
5. Roberta Flack, *First Take,* Atlantic 8230

**Art: An Illumination of
How We Carry Our
History in the Collective
Unconscious**

1. General concepts
   a. Influence of political, sociological, and psychological factors on art
   b. Revolt against classicism's ultimate order and serenity and early twentieth century romanticism
2. Character of modern art
   a. Social-realist in content
   b. Influence of primitive West Africa and South Pacific on form
3. Social and political protests
   a. Ben Shahn, *Sacco and Vanzetti*
   b. Pablo Picasso, *Guernica*
4. Movements in modern painting
   a. Fauvism and Expressionism
      1. Henri Matisse
      2. Georges Rouault
   b. Buddhism and Futurism: Pablo Picasso
   c. Dadaism
      1. Reaction against reason
      2. Nihilistic Art
      3. Cult of the absurd, the meaningless
   d. Surrealism
      1. Shock through paradox
      2. Freudian accents
      3. Examples
         (a) Salvador Dali
         (b) Paul Klee
5. Student reports: views of life
   a. Emily Dickinson
   b. John Keats
   c. Sigmund Freud and Carl Jung
   d. D. H. Lawrence
   e. Ariadne and the Minotaur (Myth of the Hero; see *The Hero with a Thousand Faces* by Joseph Campbell)

Readings, Films, Field Trips for Enrichment

1. Fiction
a. Saul Bellow, *Herzog*
b. Albert Camus, *The Stranger,* "The Guest"

c. Anton Chekhov, "A Gentleman Friend"
d. Ralph Ellison, *The Invisible Man*
e. Langston Hughes, selection from *Simple*
f. James Joyce, *A Portrait of the Artist as a Young Man*
g. Franz Kafka, *The Trial, Metamorphosis, The Penal Colony*
h. John Knowles, *A Separate Peace*
i. Arthur Koestler, *Darkness at Noon*
j. Ann Petry, *The Street*
k. J. D. Salinger, *Catcher in the Rye*
l. Jean-Paul Sartre, *No Exit*
m. Jean Toomer, *Cane*
n. John Updike, *Rabbit, Run*
o. Tennessee Williams, *The Glass Menagerie, A Streetcar Named Desire*

2. Nonfiction

a. James Baldwin, "Notes of a Native Son," "Stranger in the Village"
b. Erich Fromm, *The Art of Loving*
c. Alex Haley and Malcolm X, *Autobiography of Malcolm X*

3. Drama

a. Samuel Beckett, *Waiting for Godot*
b. Anton Chekhov, *The Three Sisters*
c. Henrik Ibsen, *The Doll's House*
d. Eugene Ionesco, *Rhinoceros*
e. Harold Pinter, *Birthday Party*

4. Films

a. *Nothing But a Man*
b. *Black Heritage Is Us*
c. *The Cool World*
d. *Oedipus*
e. *Macbeth*
f. *David and Lisa*
g. *I Have a Dream*
h. *Choice of Weapons*
i. *Intruder in the Dust*

5. Field Trips

a. Corcoran Gallery of Art
b. National Art Gallery
c. The African Museum
d. The Smithsonian Institution
e. The New Thing
f. Theaters (Film and Drama)
g. Embassies
h. The Kennedy Center

And There Are Still Other Ways

If your students are those for whom the medium is the message, an introduction to humanities through films may be the way to involve them. In addition to those films already mentioned in this chapter, a humanities program can begin with *Night and Fog, Nobody Waved Goodbye, The Wild Ones, A Short Vision,* and others.[6] Nearly every issue of *Media and Methods* suggests films which may be used to initiate or to supplement a humanities program; *Media and Methods'* articles also name many paperback books which the teacher and students can use together after viewing and discussing a film. *Hooked on Books* lists more books of this type.[7]

A humanities program can begin with a consideration of great paintings or music. Try Picasso's *Guernica,* followed by the war poems mentioned earlier in this chapter. Send or take your students to art galleries and see which works they prefer. Start from there. A social studies discussion or an editorial like the one about My Lai might begin it all. The point is that there is no "right" way to begin with every group. Your students will reveal to you where they must begin, but you must make the effort to find out who they are, what they want and need, how they can be involved in discovering themselves and the world of man. Then, with Shakespeare and with your students, you can say, "What a piece of work is man![8]

Students can make their own films, collections of photographs, or artistic pieces of work instead of or in addition to discussing or writing papers in response to the great ideas they encounter in this work.

Thomas Briggs has two appropriate quotations:

> The social concept of the humanities begins with "Know Thyself," so strongly emphasized by Socrates. Unless one has made an honest effort to know himself, there is no certainty that he can know anything else clearly; no person can be thought to be humanistically educated unless he has made serious efforts to realize what are his own potentialities in order to direct his efforts toward satisfying goals and at the same time avoiding frustrations and discouraging failures.[9]

If we want to help students in a humanities program meet and know themselves, we must be prepared to meet and know ourselves. We must ask

---

[6] Use of these films is discussed in Peter G. Kontos and James J. Murphy, *Teaching Urban Youth: A Source Book in Urban Education* (New York: John Wiley, 1967).

[7] Daniel N. Fader and Elton B. McNeil, *Hooked on Books: Program & Proof* (New York: Berkley Publishing, 1966).

[8] William Shakespeare, *Hamlet,* Act II, Scene 2. (This passage has been used as the lyric for a duet in "Hair," the rock-musical. Using both Shakespeare's play and the same idea expressed in a contemporary medium is another example of relating literature to your students' everyday experiences in a way they will identify with.)

[9] Thomas Briggs, "Reflections of a Humanist," *Relevance and the Humanities.*

ourselves the questions we ask our students and require of ourselves much more knowledge and understanding than we require of them.

> Understanding of self is essential to the understanding of others, especially of those with whom one is or should be associated, with groups of several kinds, intimate and in varying degrees remote, social and political, national and international. Literature, history, and the other social subjects properly used can powerfully contribute to understanding of other people as well as of self. International relationships could be bettered and results that are costly and often disastrous could be avoided if the humanities laid more emphasis on human relationships.[10]

To that last sentence I would add that relationships within a country—within this country—can be improved if teachers and students who now fail to understand themselves and others can begin to do so through an appreciation of the humanities.

Yet, in another article in the *Teachers College Record,* Sheila Schwartz says:

> The group of students that is in greatest need of the humanities is not getting them. I refer to the disadvantaged; that is, the group of students with little or no chance of exposure to the values of the humanities in their past, present, or future lives outside of school. Ironically, the humanities is in great need of these students if this area is to be a source of change and relevance in the curriculum and not merely a reordering of the liberal arts.[11]

In a relevant humanities program, says Schwartz, students are provided with vital dramatic experiences: a film about prejudice, a painting expressing reverence toward nature, a moving symphony written by a great composer going deaf. These provide the first essential *point of view,* "providing students with their experiences through the arts, then provoking and guiding discussion. . . . The method is inductive, or Socratic, proceeding from an immediate experience which the class has in common—a painting, film, symphony—to generalizations they can make about that experience."[12]

Especially interesting is Schwartz's second essential: *a better setting.* Many schools are either old, ugly ghetto schools or new, sterile, uninspiring cages of steel and glass. Little that is truly human can be found in either. This article suggests that better settings can be found, and I agree. Classrooms can be improved, of course, with paintings, photographs, rugs (these *are* possible), music, and the artistic expressions of your students. But you can be ingenious and can take your students for lessons to museums, art galleries, embassies, universities, and libraries. The Smithsonian Institution in Washington offers

---

[10] *Ibid.*
[11] Sheila Schwartz, "The Humanities and the Disadvantaged," in the *Teachers College Record.*
[12] *Ibid.*

classroom space. Investigate the community and see what is possible. The High School Without Walls, in Washington, D.C., is doing just this.

The third and last essential suggested in this article is that the course must *originate in the real needs* of the students and not in your head or in the heads of other curriculum planners.

> And the humanities teacher must be as skilled at eliciting and encouraging honest talk as the psychoanalyst. Teachers must have an unfaltering belief that there is value in student talk—perhaps the basic value of a humanities course.[13]

This is vital.

How to End

This chapter opened with some suggestions about how to begin; we could be tidy and finish the chapter with suggestions on how to end. Don't. An end to a humanities course is exactly what we must avoid. The experiences you initiate should be a real beginning, a continuum, a springboard for other experiences. Leave the unit without finality, completeness, or totality. If being human is the end we seek, we must not seek an ending.

---

[13] *Ibid.*

8

They Can Compose— Anything

Composition means more than the act of writing or its product. Most English teachers focus on writing to the exclusion of the other areas. We may feel incompetent in the other areas. Excellent. We can use that feeling of incompetence to understand how our students feel when they think themselves incapable of writing, and we can use the D.T.A. to let them show us what they can do well.

Begin with questions to learn what your students feel about composing and what they think it is. Discover their interests and capacities. For example, you might fill the room with many different kinds of composition: some paragraphs, essays, or poems prepared by you or by members of the class; sheet music or records to represent musical compositions; paintings, montages, collages, and sculpture to show art composition; even compound words like "bootblack" to represent the composition of words. Ask students how many compositions they recognize in the room. (Do not say "see," because the music can be played.) If they name only the written kinds, attempt through questioning to get them to realize that there are many kinds of compositions.

If you are working with students who are unwilling to try written composition because they have failed at it too often, because teachers have red-inked errors and have not recognized excellent content, or because they really do not write well, it might be best to start composition in another way. Remember that you must consider the learning styles of your students as well as your teaching style when you select a way to begin work in composition. Remember, too, that the ones I list are only suggestions.

Suggestions for Starting

Earlier questioning in the humanities area may have revealed a great deal of interest in the question, "What, if anything, is worth dying for?" Again, make available photographs, paintings, books, newspaper articles, and other items related to the subject. Try to include some objects representing the answers they have given. For example, pictures of families, a map of the U.S.A., an American flag, a baby, the Statue of Liberty, books and newspapers representing freedom of speech. Ask whether they understand what is represented, then divide the class into small groups to develop written lists of what they consider worth dying for. A recorder from each group should report to the class as a whole, and each group will then prepare a composition—written, musical, photographed, or painted—on its consensus.

Using a similar idea of great interest to the class, provide a mass of materials of many kinds for the initial preparation of rough compositions in class. These must be refined later—at home or in shop, music, or art classes. Materials should include composition paper, pens, pencils, drawing paper, crayon, charcoal, clay, soap, wood, cloth, perhaps a guitar, or whatever you and they can provide. Use a theme, a poem, a question, or a cartoon to involve the class in discussion followed by composition in the various media. "What is worth living for?" might elicit discussion about love, friendship, and other composition topics.

Discuss Shakespeare's *Romeo and Juliet* and provide illustrations of the many kinds of compositions which have grown from the original idea, including opera, ballet, and *West Side Story. Pygmalion, The Odyssey,* or the story of Icarus can be discussed in the same way, relating other versions in other art forms to the original version.

These initial experiences are intended to lead students to write, not force them to write. Neither permissiveness nor unplanned teaching is being recommended here. You must expect students to put their best efforts into whatever they compose initially; and if they begin with writing or move into it, the goal is excellence—excellence through diversity.

Composition is the culmination of all the other experiences students have shared. This is not to say that composition should come only at the end of an English course; it should be inextricably woven into their experiences in language, language arts, literature, and the humanities. Composition, though, does give the student a chance to prepare a kind of reaction that is more permanent than discussion can be; for unless discussion is recorded, exciting though it may be, it is lost. A composition can be kept, studied, revised, improved, even destroyed and prepared again.

Creative Compositions

Here are some specific creative composition ideas:

Happenings

Your students may not be verbal, may never be interested in writing a great deal, may need help in being concise, or may have short attention spans.

Discuss happenings—brief episodes which affect one deeply—with them. Use leading questions or photographs to get them into topics like these:

> The horrible moment when I saw my friend wearing a swastika.
> I took off my coat and found I had forgotten my skirt.
> Anybody could have caught that ball—but I missed.
> I was only on the phone for a minute; then I heard someone crying.

Now ask each student to write a short, one-paragraph "happening" based on some incident of his own. This should not take long, and any number of activities can be used as follow up. Papers may be exchanged so the happenings can be shared. Several can be written on the board or on transparencies. They can be read aloud, in small groups or to the whole class. Some can be role-played, dramatized with lights and sounds, or filmed. Several can be put together and produced as a "super happening."

To provide evaluation and to give students a chance to improve, collect the happenings and select one or more to reproduce and pass out or show on a transparency for class discussion.

Students may select the best happenings and have these rewritten or typed for bulletin board display. If these happenings are recorded at intervals throughout the year and kept in individual folders, students will be able to see their progress.

Prepare your own happenings, just as your students do. If you feel insecure about their quality, do not identify them as your own. See how students react to what you write first.

Collections of Student Work

Building collections of student work usually requires more planning than happening exercises do, and the bulk of this planning should be done by students. You may want to work with a group of colleagues to help your students produce a school anthology, or you may submit student work to city, state, or national collections. Here, however, we are discussing *class* anthologies—anthologies composed of creative compositions prepared by students to contain their own work.

If your class decides with you early in the year to have a collection as a culmination of the year's work, you have a goal toward which many of them will work—and everything you do in class can lead toward this: the questions, language experience stories, photographs, drawings, poems, reactions to literary selections—anything that can be seen and compiled. Cardozo High School's work is this kind of effort (first the roughly mimeographed book, *Just Rappin';* then the printed boxed work, *Cardozo Raps*). *Flamingo 1969,* done at McClymonds High School in Oakland, California, is another such student work; here are some haiku that appeared in it:

How I hate this class
On a cold winter morning
I think I'll cut it.

Elvin Tyler '71

An unhappy day
I sit alone in my room
With no dreams at all.

Bonita Cooper '71

Great birds in the sky
Looking at small things below
Insignificant!

Diane Jackson '71

How are you so sure
A man looks down from the moon . . .
Have you been up there?

Brenda McMahan '71[1]

The haiku is brief, structured, and can compress a good deal of meaning into its three lines. Students frequently enjoy this form. Here is a longer poem.

Darkness

Alone
Playing with stars
Sliding over the Milky Way
A distant comet scurries on toward the sun
A big and small dipper
But what is this?
Who dares to disturb my fortress of darkness
Inflamed with the stars of brilliant eyes
Who but man should send a ship
Sailing gracefully into a planet of wonder
It's time for me to move on
Toward another corner of
Darkness [2]

Everything in the anthology need not be poetry. The following story from *Flamingo* can evoke many images. One assumes this is a pumpkin—but perhaps it isn't.

[1] Elvin Tyler, Bonita Cooper, Diane Jackson, and Brenda McMahan, in *Flamingo 1969*, McClymonds High School, Oakland, Calif.
[2] Ozzie Anderson, "Darkness," in *Flamingo 1969*, McClymonds High School, Oakland, Calif.

House Boy

They choose me from my brothers. "This is the nicest one," they say. They take me in the house, carve me out a face. But I do not really smile until they stick a candle in my head. Then they stick me in the wild wind to be seen.

This poem by JoAnne Harris is from *Cardozo Raps.*

The Game

So I slip back into my existence. Hardly missed, hardly changed to some. But to those to whom I reveal myself a slight difference is made, because I reveal myself completely to only a few. My existence is like a great big game, two limbs on a tree. I wonder how it would be if all the world lived like you and me—minus the games and acts and things, or at least those that are very necessary, and don't matter. It wouldn't work unless people had identical personalities. But a lot of the games are unnecessary, especially the ones that hurt.[3]

There is meaning, then, not only in the written piece of work, but in its form. This is the kind of creative composition you may find your own students quite capable of doing.

JoAnne has other pieces in the anthology. For example:

The Refused

The childish
the rejected
forlorn
lost
hideous
ignorant
poor.

The neurotic
the psychotic
addicted
uncouth
crude
strange
perverted.
All of them!
Are these the outcasts?
But why?
Who are the *in*casts?
Who are the judges?[4]

[3] JoAnne Harris, "The Game," in *Cardozo Raps,* Cardozo High School, Washington, D.C.
[4] JoAnne Harris, "The Refused," in *Cardozo Raps,* Cardozo High School, Washington, D.C.

And there are these, by David Smith:

Police

What are they for?
They say they are for protection,
But it seems they do all the killing.

Untitled

We stop, look, at each other
facing a dying nation.

Countries racing to see who can
build the biggest bomb. Who shall win?

And when they have a bomb bigger
than any known, what will become
of the human race?[5]

In Herbert R. Kohl's *Teaching the Unteachable,* observe what Kohl says about the teacher's reaction to the poems by Nellie and Mary. Although this book is for teachers of children probably younger than the ones you will meet, remember that a number of your students will be uninvolved when they reach you precisely because they have had such teachers. Read what Holt and Kohl say, but pay special attention to the students' writing.[6]

In Chapter III of John Dixon's *Growth Through English,* pay particular attention to the writings on pages 46–69 in "An Analysis of Activities in Class."[7]

Newspapers or Magazines

Perhaps some of your students are more interested in newspaper or magazine writing. Since you and they will have to know something about journalism, here is a chance for you to learn with them if you do not already know

---

[5] David Smith, "Police" and "Untitled," in *Cardozo Raps,* Cardozo High School, Washington, D.C.

[6] Herbert R. Kohl, *Teaching the Unteachable,* introduction by John C. Holt. New York: New York Review, 1967.

[7] John Dixon, *Growth Through English.* A report based on the Dartmouth Seminar, 1966. Reading English National Association for the Teaching of English, 1967.

about this writing style. Don't pretend to stay one step ahead. They will catch up, so admit from the first that you must learn together if you do not know (another opportunity for the D.T.A.). Learn to write; then write news stories, editorials, or features and permit interested students to do cartoons and photographs.

Making up the newspaper is an exercise in composition. And headline writing requires specific skills.

In journalism, reading is effectively related to writing. You and your students can bring newspapers to class. Analyze the kinds of writing. Notice with students how the headlines have in them the main ideas, and how the supporting details diminish in importance from the lead paragraph to the end of the news story. Observe how differently a news story, a feature story, and an editorial will treat the same information. And observe with your students how different papers handle the same story in different ways. Your students may even want to have liberal and conservative papers—and they must read them carefully to see the differences.

Literature can lead to the preparation of newspapers. If students are reading Shakespeare's *Julius Caesar,* for example, they can compose papers written as though Caesar had just been assassinated. I remember doing this with my students long before the killings of the Kennedys and of Martin Luther King, Jr. Students found old papers with the stories about the assassination of Abraham Lincoln and brought the death of Julius Caesar up to that time. Today, such work is even more meaningful.

These papers can be done by hand and then copied, or they may be mimeographed or printed. If they are shared with other classes, a great deal can be done to inspire other such reading and composition activities in your school.

Drama

Plays must be composed before they can be acted. Composition is essential whether it is done mentally or in writing, and it involves language, form, and structure. Perhaps students would like to work in groups to prepare and present original one-act plays. Perhaps they would like to put into dramatic form something from another genre. Or perhaps the entire class wants to be involved in a more ambitious undertaking, perhaps a three-act play. No matter what the vehicle, the composition must involve some writing, some making of costumes and scenery, and some stagecraft. Again, you may have to learn with them, and again, this is a good technique.

I recall one specific dramatization that involved a group of so-called "slow" woodwork majors in the ninth grade. We were reading Dickens' *Great Expectations,* and my students were especially interested in Pip's encounter with the convict. They wanted to dramatize it, and, although the entire class was never involved, a group selected the pages to be dramatized, wrote a script—including sound effects—made a set with tombstones, and rehearsed diligently. Because I taught an "honors" class that was also studying Dickens, I decided with the students that we would present the dramatizations prepared by each class for the entire student body. The shop class did a better dramatization than the other group, and since this was a rather unexpected outcome for me at that time, I have never forgotten it.

Perhaps there is no moral to be drawn from the story I just told except that previously uninvolved students, caught up in something that interests them and trusted by a teacher who believes in them, can show what has really been there all the while. The composition and dramatization of an original play is another kind of all-involving activity that might serve to reveal intelligence and capability.

Perhaps this is the place to digress again and to say that I agree with James S. Coleman that "schools must not have as their primary goal the teaching of children." Children enter school, says Coleman, loaded with information from television and other media.[8] I must add that they also come loaded with information from their diverse cultures. What the student needs, says Coleman, is not more information but "opportunity for responsible productive action, for any action that tests and develops him."

The kinds of creative composition discussed here, and others that you will discover for yourselves, will test and develop the student, not rejecting what he has but challenging him to use it, to hone and polish it, to present it as his to others who will respect him for it and will know that he has something to say.

Of course, students, like the rest of us, will continue to need information. But if one knows where and how to get the information he wants and needs, if one knows how to learn, the "what" is easy, and the sources are there. Preparation of a dramatic work of any kind will demand that teacher and students go to the right sources, find necessary information, analyze needs, use what is needed, reject what is not needed (for the moment at least), and call on the skills and talents and working ability of many people working cooperatively to produce—to compose—a suitable piece of work. And that piece of work will be a composition.

Musical Productions

There is little more to say about the musical production as a composition that has not already been said about the drama, except that of course the music

[8] James S. Coleman, speech given on December 1970 to the School of Advanced International Studies at Johns Hopkins University. Dr. Coleman is professor of social relations at Johns Hopkins University.

must be composed. Here again is an opportuntity for the D.T.A. if you do not know music. Many students, including great numbers of those who are apparently uninterested in school, do know music.

Several years ago I remember seeing an imaginative teacher, Mary Turner, working with *Julius Caesar* in a class. One day, a student who was very much interested in music came to class with a musical opus called "The Assassination of Julius Caesar." This was certainly a musical composition. This teacher elicited from her students a great deal of work of this kind. There was a production of *Julius Caesar* with puppets and music, of "The Ancient Mariner," and of other works of literature.

In the last chapter, I dealt with the understanding and appreciation of music as part of the humane side of man's nature. Here, I am concerned with its production. Much can come from exposing students to the kinds of music cited in that chapter. It might so capture and fire their imaginations that they will themselves compose and thus become involved.

Films

Very young students in Washington have been turned loose with inexpensive cameras to make and develop their own photographs. This process is composition, and it usually leads to discussion and writing. Your students can become involved in such composition also.

A number of elementary and secondary school teachers have begun experimenting with student-made films. Again, I am moving away from the use of films made by others to the process of composing such films by students. At the Princeton–Trenton Institute for Teachers of the Disadvantaged in the summer of 1966, a group of students produced a remarkably good film, with sequence, trick shots, and even "happenings" on film. In Washington, D.C., in 1969 a group of high school students in a humanities program produced films, instead of writing papers in response to readings. These, too, are excellent compositions. Another group of junior high school students here also produced a film under the guidance of their English teacher, Delores Kendrick, who had worked the year before in a private school for boys in Hawaii where the students produced films. Many teachers, in this city and in others, have begun to see work with film as composition.

The uninvolved student, who for years has failed with pen or pencil to make himself understood, may be adept at using a camera to compose. He should at least be given a chance to use a medium because although he may feel uneasy with literature or reading, he has been familiar with photographs all his life. It may suit his learning style and may make him more willing, finding success and acceptance, to use other modes—even writing—later on.

Incidentally, the animated film and the nonobjective or abstract film must not be neglected as possibilities here. Very young children have learned to animate, and surely there may be older children who would like to try it.

The film is probably the most elaborate kind of composition, since if it is to be complete a script must be written, music must be composed and sound effects devised, and the filming is itself composing. Then all of these must be synchronized to produce a finished composition.

9

The Medium as Method

me'-di-um, n.; pl. mediums or media . . . something in a middle position; a means of conveying or effecting something; a channel of communication; go-between, intermediary; an individual held to be a channel of communication between the earthly world and the world of spirits.

These five definitions of media complement my own ideas about the *uses* of media. But perhaps a few questions will clarify them.

Should you, the teacher, be the essential medium?

Are you and the students the only real requirements for learning?

Do you (like Socrates) plus the right questions and a receptive student equal real learning?

Is there something else that can do the job as well as you can? Or can that "something else" only help? This may be more relevant than you think. By using media, can you do a better job or multiply your usefulness?

You know yourself and your learning and teaching styles. You know that you must discover the learning styles of your students. Only then can you use materials besides yourself and your students; only then can you move to media.

The Definitions Extended

In one sense, you are the medium. You are "in the middle position" between your students and learning. Your thoughtful questions and their answers show you what they need and want to learn. Of the things that are around you, what can you use to help each individual learn better? What media can assist you in diagnosing needs? Chalkboard? Overhead projector? Tape recorder? Videotape?

Because you and your students must "convey information" to and from each other, what media can best facilitate this? Filmstrips? Cameras? Tele-trainers? Record players? Opaque projectors?

You and your students are "major channels of communication" with each other and with persons outside of the classroom. You are both receivers and senders. Can you use media to improve these communicative channels? Radio? Television? Journals? Newspapers? Films?

The intermediary, the go-between is *you.* Can you use another medium to serve this function, while you act as a silent observer of interaction among your students? For example, can you tape a story with a problem ending to be role-played? Can you tape a set of directions to be followed by your class as you watch? Will these media help? Record player? Tape recorder? Cassette tape? Film loop?

Finally, you are "a channel of communication between the earthly world and the world of spirits." True learning is an intangible—it is of the spirit—and the uninvolved student is often one who has been earthbound by those who have tried to teach him only vocational skills.

Five Uses of Media

There are five focal points for discussing media: (1) using media for diagnosis, (2) using media for individualized instruction, (3) using media for improving the self-image of the uninvolved student, (4) using media for evaluation by students and by the teacher, and (5) using media to extend the necessarily limited services of the teacher.

Using Media for Diagnosis

Problem.   Your students are so uninterested in their English class that they seldom come. They have underlined so many subjects and predicates, drearily diagrammed so many sentences, tiredly listed so many parts of speech, and have been accused of having lazy lips and tongues so often that they are afraid to undergo such torture again. You want to find out what their real needs and interests are so you can provide a climate for learning, can plan effectively with and for them, can share with them your knowledge of what English really is and your faith in their ability to learn it.

Method without media.   You sit in a small circle with those of your students who do venture into the room, and you ask questions. You look directly at them and attempt to engage their interest through your own interest in them. Perhaps you share with them some of your own interests and needs. As you listen, you make mental notes about what they say they want to know. But you also listen to their ways of expressing themselves: their language, their choice of words, their use of nonstandard English, their speech and usage. You look for nonverbal indications: for silent students, for gestures, for facial expressions.

Method with media.   A tape recorder, possibly an inconspicuous one using cassettes, can be a valuable medium for diagnosis. Since the answers to your questions are recorded, you can study the language and answers at your leisure or when you devise lessons to meet students' needs. Also, since you are taping, you can devote less time to close listening and more to observation of nonverbal behavior. Videotape, if available, can record verbal as well as nonverbal behavior for later diagnosis by students and teacher. Closed-circuit television can place you outside the room as an observer, with students responding to your taped questions, or to questions put by an intern, a paraprofessional, or a student.

Using Media for
Individualizing Instruction

Problem.   Your heterogeneously grouped class is driving you up the wall because so many levels of ability are represented. In reading, for example, you must provide books on many levels and must whirl like a dervish to get around to the many groups. Then, there are individuals who should be working with you alone, either because they are way ahead of the others or are far behind—perhaps reading at second grade level in an eleventh grade class.

Method without media.   Using group dynamics techniques, you divide the class, and each group selects a leader. You move around as well as you can, helping the leaders and working with those students who require your attention.

Method with media.   You use the communications laboratory which has many ways to provide for individual differences in reading, or you use some of these materials in your classes:

An individual tachistoscope (an apparatus for the brief exposure of visual stimuli) operated by the student may help him improve his reading rate, vocabulary, and comprehension.

Readers of various kinds which show stories or other material on filmstrips can be used individually or by small groups.

Tape recorders for "listen and read" exercises can be used individually or in small groups. Earphones can provide privacy and will keep these students from interfering with the work of others.

Programmed materials involving books or machines are useful for some students. You know the learning styles of your students; and those who learn best this way should be free to do so.

Individuals or pairs of students read to a tape recorder. Later, you can check these readings, but you are free to observe while the activity goes on.

Improving Self-Image Through Media

Problem.   For years, many of your uninvolved students have seen themselves only through the eyes of others—others who too often saw them in a negative light. Now you want to help them see themselves in positive ways. Perhaps a Humanities program can help.

Method without media.   Begin in the world of your students with a work like Margaret Walker's *Jubilee.* Read parts of this work with your students and add to it other poems, essays, music, and art which will help them to see the theme or idea of common humanity in the work. James Weldon Johnson's *God's Trombones,* spirituals, jazz, blues, slave narratives, the Brady Civil War photographs, short stories by Ambrose Bierce, Walt Whitman's poetry—all these and many others can be used. Is this enough?

Method with media.   Black students who have never really seen themselves as human beings in the literature, history, and life of this country must do more than simply read the works cited above. They must hear records and tapes of spirituals, jazz, and blues; see films like *A Raisin in the Sun* and documentaries; observe themselves on closed-circuit television and videotape while they are role playing or engaged in creative drama. Students who have felt inept in verbal situations but who are competent in technical matters can improve their image of themselves by installing and operating the audiovisual equipment. Those students who prefer doing so may want to make their own films, photographs, or tapes.

Using Media for Evaluation

Problem.   You want an accurate evaluation of your students —more than a simple test of their progress in learning English content. You understand evaluation to be the constant process of seeing where we are now, where we are going, and whether we are getting better or worse at learning. Questions and tests can, of course, be used, but the evaluation of compositions seems best.

Method without media.   Brief "happenings" can be written, journals can be kept, expository or creative writing can be done. You can take home hundreds of papers and can spend many hours reading and evaluating them. You may even have a lay reader or a student assist you. Is this the best possible way to evaluate or to help students learn to evaluate for themselves?

Method with media.   Evaluation of compositions lends itself beautifully to the use of media. Try writing your own composition which incorporates those ideas you would like your students to focus on. These can include either good or bad features in their own writing. Duplicate these and pass them out for small-group or even individual analysis, discussion, and rewriting. Or use a transparency and the overhead projector for class analysis and evaluation. Overlays can be used to give alternatives or to point up—perhaps in color—those things you want to emphasize.

Compositions can be put on tape and heard at listening posts by individuals or by the whole class. Punctuation and mechanics of this kind sometimes can be improved if a composition is heard, since punctuation often depends on stress, pitch, and juncture.

Other kinds of compositions can be filmed, photographed, videotaped, televised via closed circuits, painted, and otherwise prepared for a more detailed evaluation by you and by student creators and evaluators, or even by outside expert consultants.

Using Media as Teacher-Extender

Problem.   No teacher knows all; no teacher can do all or be all to his students. The classroom with the teacher serving *only* as a lecturer in any or all aspects of English is outmoded. You must work on a one-to-one basis with many "unhooked" students who believe that they dislike literature.

Method without media.   In a literature class—possibly the last outpost of the lecturer—the classroom is filled with colorful and relevant books, and you are a well-prepared teacher.

Method with media.   Begin with a classroom filled with colorful and involving books, but use films and filmstrips to motivate, to "hook," and to get students *into* the books. It is not necessary to use long feature films, or even to show films for an entire class. Film loops and 8mm projectors—or even individually shown films—can individualize presentations and can extend the services of the teacher. They can show what the teacher may not have seen or even imagined: the Greek world, Africa, Mark Twain's Mississippi River, or Gordon Parks' homeland.

Use records and tapes of poems and short stories, or use those records which tell—with sound effects—a story up to a high point of interest, in order to "hook" students into finishing. Use these media also to tell stories which set problems to be solved through role-playing. If you are not especially dramatic, you are extending yourself through media if

Ruby Dee, Ossie Davis, Richard Burton, or other actors and actresses can do the reading for you.

In a sense, then, the use of media will provide another teacher for your classroom; it will extend your services to your students so that you can play your role more effectively.

10 Planning for Action

No discussion of how to plan for action makes sense unless it takes first things first. And the first thing is *you*. I must be quite clear about your role. It is essential that you understand, accept, and respect yourself before you go to work with your students. What we have said about the goals of students is equally applicable to you.

You have control of the language and can make it work well for you, although you will never know everything about it.

You have mastered quite a lot of the content of English; you realize that you can be a resource for your students. You will not lecture them but will share with them, using methods possibly from this book, from other books, and methods you will create.

You know your style: enthusiastic or controlled, organized or spontaneous. (You understand that you will use your teaching style and will adapt methods to suit you and your students.)

You have confidence in yourself as a human being who is prepared to involve other human beings in the fascinating process of learning. (You know that all young children enjoy learning, and that somehow the students you will work with have been turned off. You can rekindle that desire to learn.)

You know other things about yourself, including some weaknesses. (You have seen that every human being has weaknesses, and that every human being—teacher and student—has strengths.)

Behavioral Goals

There is a great deal of discussion now about behavioral goals. Some English professors and teachers have rejected them for our discipline, insisting that to use them is to place teachers and students in straitjackets. They say that student behavior in English cannot, or should not, be measured. They may be right, but before you decide for yourself, be sure you have heard both sides of the controversy.[1]

Certainly in the affective areas of English you will find it difficult to measure changes in student behavior. It may be possible, however, to see and to measure differences in the cognitive areas. The appendixes to this chapter contain sample lessons and other material prepared for your analysis and possible use. See "Appendix A: Behavioral Goals for a Language/Communications Class." Discuss these goals with your colleagues, but try to avoid settling into any fixed point of view about them until you have given them a fair chance.

Teaching Styles

A great deal of your success with the uninvolved depends on your recognizing your best teaching style and not attempting to imitate someone else who appears to be using certain methods successfully. They might never work for you. You may find your own teaching styles among those listed below.

URA (utterly relaxed always). You—man or woman, young or old—are like a piece of cooked spaghetti. You are calm and relaxed and find it easy to teach perched on a table, shoeless, or sitting among the students. As long as you are not just *pretending,* but are truly like this innately, you can do an enviable job of getting and building student confidence. Techniques in this book that work especially well for a teacher like this are the questioning and discovery methods, use of role playing and photographs, helping students keep journals, arranging for improvisations and happenings. Often, this URA teacher is not at all interested in structured behavioral goals or in machines. You are not only able but anxious to use the D.T.A. There may be some overlap with another style, though, so nothing I say here is a rule in any sense if this is you.

RAT (relaxed at times—sorry about that anagram). Often utterly relaxed like the URA, at other times you feel the need for more structure and plan carefully for each day's work. You are, however, flexible enough to abandon the plan instantly when you see it is not working. Questioning, acceptance, and the inductive approaches come easily to you, but you are probably more willing to prepare materials (perhaps mimeographed) and to use the overhead projector, tape recorder, and a few other machines occasionally. Yours is a student-centered class, but you are less likely to use the D.T.A. than the URA teacher, whom nothing threatens. Not as secure with improvisation and role playing, you are probably willing to use creative drama and rehearsed dramati-

---

[1] I suggest you read Robert F. Mager, *Preparing Instructional Objectives* (Belmont, Calif.: Fearon, 1961, 1967) and Arnold Leslie Lazarus, *Selected Objectives for the English Language Arts* (Boston: Houghton Mifflin, 1967). Study the report of the committee on Behavioral Goals in English. Be sure to read James Moffett's objections to such goals.

zation in class. You will help students make collections of their compositions and will see that these are produced and distributed in some way.

BAD (bubbly and dramatic—sorry, the initials didn't turn out so well here, either; however, if you know what young people mean when they use this term, you may feel better). You are an extroverted and dramatic person. You might have become a stage or television personality if you had not decided on teaching. Oral interpretation for and with students is something you enjoy, as you do every aspect of drama: improvisations, creative dramatics, role playing, choral readings, writing and producing plays, and films. Avoid being the constant center of attention; since you can act, sometimes act quiet and retiring. You may enjoy using all media but may have difficulty with the D.T.A.

BOP (beautifully organized person). There is little I need to say to or about you, because you have studied this book, made careful notes, read all of the references, again made careful notes, and will use all that you have read and inferred as you plan for your students. Keep doing this and include students in your planning. Don't try to be URA, RAT, or a BAD. You are a BOP.

There are other teaching styles, of course. Think about some of the best teachers you have ever had; if they do not fit into the categories listed here or are not a composite of several of these categories, analyze their teaching styles in retrospect. Discuss excellent teachers with your colleagues, friends, and families to see if you can find still other styles. Think, also, about books you have read and films you have seen about teaching. There are, for example, *To Sir, With Love, Up the Down Staircase, Blackboard Jungle,* and even *Goodbye, Mr. Chips.*

Planning

There is no point in my just talking about planning; you need to know what to do. Let us assume that you will be teaching American studies at the eighth or eleventh grade levels. (Even though you may have an eleventh grade class, the interest and reading levels as well as language difficulties may force you to use some materials actually prepared for eighth grade use.) You must begin to plan before you meet your students. Ask these questions:

Has the chronological arrangement of American studies usually worked? Can it "hook" uninvolved students? Is there a better way to organize the year (or term)? What materials are available?

Textbooks? How are they organized?

Pictures? How can they be used?

Films? Are they easily available?

Supplementary books, especially about misrepresented or neglected aspects of American and other cultures? Can you get these? Should you begin with contemporary ideas and work back into the past as you follow these ideas?

Can you use behavioral goals? How?

In what ways can you integrate language, language arts, literature, humanities, and creative composition in an American studies course for the uninvolved? Consider the examples of planning that are found at the end of this chapter—"Appendix B: Course Outline for American Studies"; "Appendix C: Unit Outline for American Studies"; "Appendix D: Lesson Plans for American Studies"; and "Appendix E: Several Plans for the First Day of School."

A course dealing with basic communication skills is necessary whenever students from diverse cultures must learn how to cope with and participate in life. Some specific suggestions on objectives and activities in such a course can be found in "Appendix F: Tentative Curriculum Guide for Communications."

Planning for Teaching Reading

Of the communication skills, reading is the one most often cited to be inadequate in secondary school students, and this inadequacy is the cause of most failures in other skills. Using resources listed throughout this book and in the bibliography at the end of the book, you should be able to plan lessons.

Besides the role, attitude, and personality of the teacher and effective planning, other elements are necessary for successful teaching: good classroom management and a good learning atmosphere.

Classroom Management

A sociometric chart, or sociogram, can be made with the help of pupils, and sometimes groups can be organized on the basis the sociogram indicates. Every pupil simply writes his name on a sheet of paper and writes names of two or three classmates with whom he would like to work on a project, in a reading seminar, or in some other activity. When the teacher has collected them, the resulting chart will indicate those pupils never selected—the isolates —and those popular ones selected more often. Placing the isolated in groups with those selected most often will help both. The key people can serve as discussion leaders for whatever is being done.

Another way to group students is into triads, or group of three, by counting off. If each group has three positions (leader, recorder, silent observer) that each member must fill in turn, everyone will have a chance "to walk in someone else's shoes."

Old newspapers and magazines for reading can help individualize instruction, as can the use of different photographs and paintings for composition. Articles can be matched with pictures, headlines can be matched with articles, pupils can begin their individual journals and other creative works. And the teacher can further individualize instruction by starting a file folder for each student and asking students to start their own word files, if this class is using that method.

After a few days when the teacher has studied pupils' records, seen the contents of the folders, perhaps listened to tapes of the pupils' language, studied the sociogram described above, and maybe seen some journals, he can begin to formulate behavioral goals for each pupil. These can be quite simple and can be kept in the pupils' files, but they will guide the teacher in selecting and preparing materials.

One brief example may suffice to illustrate what I mean. A ninth grade class of 35 pupils reports at period one to Mr. X, the English teacher. After introducing himself, he passes out sheets of paper and gives simple directions for getting names, interests, and the sociometric material from each pupil. He learns immediately which pupils listen well and follow directions. He may then ask each one to write—or if he uses a tape recorder, to talk—about himself. More individual information. Instead, he may choose to use reading materials, pictures, or music to elicit further information.

When the class has gone, working out the sociogram and going over the papers and/or tapes yields still more information. Only then will he go to the office records to check out more information. (Or he may *never* go.) He knows a number of things about each pupil before the second day.

Whether he is an isolate, or an unknown, or popular.

Whether he listens and follows directions well or has a listening or language barrier.

Whether he needs help with spelling (or reading, or speaking).

Whether he just came to the city from rural Mississippi or Puerto Rico.

Whether he appears apathetic or is hyperactive.

Learning Atmosphere

Our primary interest is the uninvolved student; we cannot ignore the fact that more and more students lose interest in school every day. Some of you will hear a rationale for neglect when you begin to teach:

"We can't do anything with these kids. The parents and community have never shown an interest in education, and these students are not motivated to learn."

"The elementary schools haven't taught them anything, so how can we be expected to do it?"

"We don't get any support from the administration; the discipline is terrible;

the tardiness, truancy, and dropout rates are unbelievable; outsiders are walking the halls."

"We don't have any books, the right books, access to media, paper, decent rooms, or *anything,* so how can we teach?"

"There are no courses of study, curriculum guides, or plans and no planning time has been provided, so how do we know what to teach?"

"These students don't want to learn."

Let me help destroy these straw men by asking some questions. Some youngsters from so-called poor, deprived, and uninterested communities have always achieved. Is it not possible that with a teacher's right attitude, more can be saved? Read what James Baldwin and others have said about their teachers. Wouldn't you like to have someone say such things about you?

How can a secondary school teacher know what has been taught in elementary schools unless he visits them? Sometimes too much grammar and reading is taught rather than not enough. Why not investigate before making assumptions?

Didn't schools exist before administrators did? Did Socrates have a principal? If you do an excellent job, won't it be recognized and the necessary support given? If not, does it matter that much?

Can't you accept the nonavailability of materials as a challenge to your creativity? Have you noticed all suggestions and readings in this book which require no books, media, paper, decent rooms, or anything else?

Must you follow a plan written by someone who does not know your students as well as you do?

Don't you feel that all students want to learn? If not, you are in the wrong profession.

First, there must not be chaos. You must have planned so carefully that you feel secure. Students will feel your confidence and will react to it. Know what kinds of questions you want to ask, and why and how you intend to ask them. Know how you want the room arranged so it complements your teaching style. Later it can reflect the individual learning styles of your students. Be firm yet flexible as you begin work.

Second, do a few things well in the beginning. Begin tuning in your students with appropriate questions (which you perhaps have rehearsed and tried out on others earlier and set the tone for your work by planning, by your appropriate dress and grooming, by your nonverbal and verbal communication.

Third, the atmosphere for learning must include you and your students. If you can, let them teach you something every day. Let the books in your room, the media you use with your students, the bulletin board, even the walls, floor, and ceilings reflect the atmosphere you and your students like best. Don't wait for funds to set up a communications laboratory with carrels, hardware, and software. Let the students help you with paint, paintings, paper, newspapers, magazines, cardboard, rugs, boards and bricks (for bookcases), and anything else needed to create the right mood for all of you. This "room-making" might be one way to involve some uninterested students.

Concluding remarks are always difficult: either they restate what has already been said or they introduce new ideas that themselves need another book for adequate explanation.

In this case, I want to come full circle and remind you where we began: with a teacher fresh from a college that gave her no special preparation for the real world of the classroom; with students similarly unprepared, fresh from years of failure, indifference, or open hostility. We faced each other over chasms of mistakes, misunderstandings, and prejudice. Being a victim of prejudice does not free one from practicing it. Whatever we may have suffered as people, we cannot as teachers transmit that suffering to those other victims in our care. Just as being black did not keep me, early in my career as a teacher, from expecting middle-class white behavior from my students, being creative ourselves does not prevent us from expecting others to exhibit lock-step learning processes. In short, we must be students ourselves to teach others successfully.

Throughout this book I have tried to provide specific class activities rather than general theory. I have consistently—perhaps inconsistently—harped on the atmosphere as well as the instruction. These recommendations have worked and are working for me. But none of it could work without the one concept about our craft that is its lifeblood: that students—"they"—are people. In fact, they may be the last "true" people on earth. Their legacy from us must not be one of despair—our human and professional pride requires that it must not be so. And time is not forever. Somehow we must take the step that bridges generations, races, and cultures in order that life be livable for the heirs of the earth. Life, indeed, is the word. Education is about life, our students are life, and we must make the connection between school and their life. "Life is what happens while you are making other plans."

Appendix A: Behavioral Goals for a Language/Communications Class

These behavioral goals are meant to identify the kind of progress you would hope for from students in a language/communications class and the kind of achievement you would channel them toward. The following goals are listed in order of difficulty. Also, each goal has four levels of achievement:

1. Each student should try to reach the goal based on what he already knows about his speech and what he discerns as he speaks.
2. Students can listen to tape recordings or see videotapes of themselves for a new perspective on how well they achieve each goal.
3. Students can listen to and observe others to test their ability to discern what each goal suggests.
4. The student is not only able to detect these differences but can also describe them.

Keep these levels of achievement in mind as you read the following behavioral goals:

1. The student is able to detect differences in dialect between his speech and that of others. He recognizes all speech as some dialect of American English and is able to detect the differences between one dialect and another.
2. The student can perceive different levels of discourse:
   a. Are there any differences between the textual and subtextual message?
   b. What is the relationship between content and purpose? Content and style?
   c. Is the tone objective or subjective?
3. When the student can see as well as hear a speech (whether it's a videotape of his own speech or that of someone else), he can identify the nonverbal messages. He will observe facial expressions, gestures, and movements which mitigate or explain more fully what is said.
4. The student can make creative use of the foregoing observations:
   a. He can identify any speech that is inappropriate.
   b. He can rephrase inappropriate speech to make it appropriate for a given audience.
   c. He can shift from one level of discourse to another as the occasion warrants.
   d. He can select verbal presentations that are appropriate for a given audience, evaluating the audience's age, interests, background, purpose in listening, and other factors.
   e. He can project his voice adequately so the entire audience, whether large or small, can hear him comfortably.

Appendix B: Course Outline for American Studies

I. Life

The first part of this unit is about life in this land, starting where the learner is in the contemporary world. Read stories and poems about rural and urban areas; both music and art can contribute to an understanding of life in America today.

II. Liberty

This segment may be organized chronologically, once students have become involved in the "now." Current problems and themes have their roots in the past; these can be explored as questions like the following:

1. How and why did people come here in the first place?
2. What is "liberty"?
3. How has our literature reflected a search for freedom?
4. What freedoms have been destroyed as America developed?

III. Pursuit of Happiness

Here students can take a close look at the present, the past, and the future as they listen to music; read or hear literary works; see films, photographs, and paintings; compose, write, and discuss works of their own.

Note: This course outline is intended to be brief. You must devise your own, more complete outline on the needs and interests of your students.

Appendix C: Unit Outline for American Studies

Goals

The skillful reader can elicit several levels of meaning, direct and metaphorical, from a poem. Given a short poem or several poems, he can explicate with understanding and can interpret meanings from context clues, through analysis, or with other reading skills.

Given a body of multi-ethnic materials, the learner will begin to know his country.

Materials

Anthology

Brooks, Charlotte K., ed. *Search for America.* Level 2 of the *Impact* series. New York: Holt, Rinehart & Winston, 1968.

Supplementary Books

Adoff, A., ed. *I Am the Darker Brother: An Anthology of Modern Poems by Black Americans.* New York: Macmillan Co., 1968.

Borland, Hal G. *When the Legends Die.* Philadelphia: J. B. Lippincott Co., 1963.

Brooks, Charlotte K., ed. *The Outnumbered: Stories, Essays and Poems about Minority Groups.* New York: Delacorte Press, 1967.

Turner, M., ed. *We, Too, Belong.* New York: Dell Publishing Co., 1969.

Things to Do

Question students about the American search for life, liberty, and the pursuit of happiness after playing Phil Ochs' recording of "Power and Glory." Study the initial picture spread in *Search for America* and discuss.

Select a poem for careful inductive teaching. (In the lesson plan, I have used Hughes' "I, Too, Sing America.")

Discuss the reasons why people came to this land, and read related stories and poems in the anthology.

Read "Bear's Brother" in *When the Legends Die* and see how many students are interested in reading the entire book. (This can also be done with "Can You Forge" from Margaret Walker's *Jubilee*.)

Play Martin Luther King, Jr.'s "I Have a Dream" speech, and let students read from the book or from dittoed sheets. Discuss.

Use appropriate photographs, films, and paintings to illuminate poems and stories and to stimulate engagement.

Move now to Langston Hughes' poem "I, Too, Sing America," perhaps with some such bridging statement as, "Here is a poem about a man with a dream, written by a poet who often wrote about dreams." You may want to read or recite "Hold Fast to Dreams" or "A Dream Deferred."

Presentation

The room should be filled with pictures of "the darker brother" in America. In the final lesson on liberty, pupils' drawings should be included. Portraits of famous Americans like Peter Salem, Crispus Attucks, Frederick Douglass, Jackie Robinson, Marian Anderson, Chief Joseph, Sitting Bull, or Geronimo should be included. Also, photographs of contemporary Puerto Ricans, Orientals, Hawaiians, Alaskans, and others should be on display. The supplementary paperback books in class should be so displayed that students can see the faces of the people in the photographs.

When pupils have had a chance to see that they are surrounded by the faces of many different kinds of Americans, books that are displayed should be opened so students can look at the illustrations without comment while a record of one of the poems mentioned above is played. If no record is available, play a prepared tape or read the poem aloud.

Two questions are important here:

1. What does the poem say? Ask pupils to restate its meaning in their own words.

2. What does the poem mean? Here, pupils must draw inferences from the language of the poem. Let them work in pairs to talk about what these phrases really mean:

> the darker brother
> to eat in the kitchen
> at the table
> how beautiful I am

A pupil may lead the discussion of what the poem means. When they reach a consensus, pupils should write a two-paragraph composition of what the poem means on a worksheet.

Follow-up

The student completes his worksheet and finds or draws a picture to illustrate it. These papers will be added to the classroom display.

Comment

When I used "I, Too, Sing America" in a ninth grade class, I wrote it on the chalkboard and asked such questions as these:

Who is the "I" in the poem? Could it be Cassius Clay? (The class corrected me by saying Muhammed Ali.) Could it be a Mississippi sharecropper? (I had a picture.)

Is "the darker brother" a slave?

When we reached the line, "They send me to eat in the kitchen when company comes," I asked whether Hughes literally meant a kitchen. At this point one student, remembering Muhammed Ali, said, "No, the 'kitchen' is any place where you can't do what you want, like boxing."

Finally, the class discussed differences between the first and last lines of the poem.

Appendix D: Lesson Plans for American Studies

Lesson Plan I: "Power and Glory" by Phil Ochs

Presentation

Play the record all the way through without commenting. Look at the faces of the listeners to see what they seem to be feeling. This is a song that speaks of the potential power and glory of a land that has "beauty that words cannot recall."

Write on the blackboard:

> Yet she's only as rich as the poorest of the poor,
> Only as free as the padlocked prison door,
> Only as strong as our love for this land,
> Only as tall as we stand.[1]

When the song has ended, read these words aloud, encouraging pupils to read with you. Ask:

What do these words mean?

How can this country be only "as rich as . . . "? "as free as . . . "? "as strong as . . . "? "as tall as . . ."?

Encourage free discussion of the meanings of these terms. Ask pupils to give orally or to write sentences with the same ideas as those in the song. It might be simple to divide them into four groups, each to develop a sentence. After about fifteen minutes, ask a member of each group to write the group's selection of the best sentence on the board, beside what you have written. Something like this might be written:

> Yet she's only as fair as the best of the people,
> Only as good as the highest church steeple,
> Only as kind as our love for this place,
> Only as free as this race.

Their efforts might be as imperfect as this, but suggestions for improvement can be made and should be accepted.

Play the song again, encouraging pupils to sing quietly with it.

Turn to the study sheet, and ask pupils to mark the places mentioned in the third stanza of "I, Too, Sing America." Work this out with them, using a map of the United States.

Follow-up

Finish marking the places on the student worksheet, coloring them and drawing illustrations in the margin if interested.

Student Worksheet

1. Outline map of the U.S.A. with dotted lines but *no names* indicating states. (Hawaii and Alaska *must* be included.)

2. Words from "Power and Glory" at top: "From Colorado, Kansas, and the Carolinas, to Virginia and Alaska, from the old to the new, Texas and Ohio and the California shore, tell me who could ask for more."

Lesson Plan II: "American Gothic" by Samuel Allen

Presentation

Play or read the poem. Can you think of other seemingly impossible things like the poem and the picture? What other Americans might say something like this?

A writing assignment, preferably done in class, is intended to sharpen pupils' powers of observation, test their close and inferential reading skills, elicit samples of their language, introduce them to the use of models for writing, and help them enjoy reading and writing poetry.

Ask them to use this poem as a model, and write one based on their own experiences, on those of another talented American, or on this illustration or others in the book. A class group poem might be developed first. For example, using the Gordon Parks photograph at the back of the anthology, something like this could be written:

> Often I feel like I will never get up
> Just lie here forever

'Til one fine afternoon
I'm gonna tie a string on a bug
Let it walk softly on my face
And feel its fine legs on my forehead
Then look up in the sky and say
This is fun!

The writing can be done individually, in pairs, in small groups, or as a total class activity.

Follow-up

Read stories about sports heroes in anthologies or in supplementary books (*I Always Wanted to Be Somebody, Go Up for Glory*). Using the model, write a poem about one of these persons.

Appendix E: Several Plans for the First Day of School

A.   Write your name on the chalkboard and stand by the door to greet students as they enter. Be sure that you took the time to arrange the room as you want it, perhaps with the chairs in a large circle, or a circle within a circle. Sit in the group, not at the desk, and introduce yourself. You might be able to go immediately into the questioning suggested earlier as one of the best ways to begin.

B.   Have a stark, empty room if your personality is strong enough to fill it. Gradually, as you learn your students' interests, encourage them to help you make the room represent them.

C.   Begin with a colorful, relevant, "alive" room, with many items that interest students. Eliminate what they reject and what you find useless. Let the room change as you discover your students' interests and as they create their own display material in language, language arts, literature, humanities, and creative composition.

Appendix F: Tentative Curriculum Guide for Communications[1]

Our major aim in this *Curriculum Guide for Communications* is to provide practical teacher assistance. Listening, speaking, reading and writing are the means of expressing and receiving ideas and emotions. While these skills cannot be separated in reality, they are separated here for convenience of objectives, stated specifically with parallel activities. These skills are common to every level of instruction and should be emphasized and expanded on each succeeding level.

Probably our greatest responsibility to students is to train their growth in all facets of interaction. Awareness is the first of these facets in communications, and sometimes this must be taught. By ascertaining what facts or ideas the pupils already know and can use, the teacher performs the double service of increasing awareness and establishing a basis for new ideas and/or facts. In this type of activity lies built-in motivation. The students are stimulated to develop *more* skills because of their increased success in handling those which they already possess.

This Guide does not provide an outline of content to be covered; instead, it supplies lists of activities leading to specific, measurable objectives.

This booklet can be used to serve as a course of study for secondary school classes in communications; as a supplement for communications laboratories; to augment the English curriculum. The imaginative teacher can surely add many ideas in all areas and can draw even more suggestions from the students themselves. Those who prepared and now distribute this guide welcome your comments and suggestions.

The items called "objectives and activities" contain activities which increase in difficulty: Level A consists of beginning skills; Level B is a little more advanced; Level C is still more advanced. This order is by no means binding and should be consolidated and adapted as needed.

Starting Tips

A. Start with yourself
(Level A)

1. Be sure your own attitude is right for the classroom. Each pupil is a person.

---

[1] *A Tentative Curriculum Guide for Communications,* prepared in spring 1968 by a committee of five teachers: Juanita L. Allen, Thelma J. Montgomery, Alma L. Rimmer, Pauline A. Smeed, and Ruby M. Thornton. Thelma H. Johnson was production chairman.

2. Keep the fine but important line between teacher and pupil. Being friendly doesn't mean being a "buddy."
3. Be sure that your appearance causes no untoward distraction.
4. Use your voice as your most important teaching tool; proper stress, pitch, emphasis indicate poise. Yelling indicates just the opposite.
5. Have every activity well planned. Try to predict pupils' responses, and be ready to cope with them.

B. Make your environment help you (Level B)

1. Have room properly lighted and ventilated.
2. Keep room attractive and appropriate for your area of teaching.
3. Keep something related to what you are teaching on display.
4. Place current, colorful, expressive pictures on bulletin board.
5. Place on blackboard, bulletin, or flannel board items needed daily: date, teacher's name, notices to students, and so on.

Floating teachers: Prepare a topical, portable bulletin on a roll similar to a window shade. Have a committee of pupils in each class help with it. Rotate duty.

C. Be able to identify pupils quickly (Level C)

1. Whether a list of pupils is given to you or not, have them make tags with name, section, seat number and row.
2. Use these to make seating charts so you can call everyone by name immediately.
3. Insist on the same seating arrangement every day unless you change it for a definite reason.
4. Note and remember individual traits.
5. Provide immediate responsibilities for as many as possible.
6. Have pupils try to recognize fulfilling their responsibilities as communication.

D. Involve pupils in every step (Level A)

1. Don't tell them; get them to tell you!
2. In making your plans, include getting pupils' ideas about each aim.
3. Include their ideas about achieving each aim.
4. Help them to realize that self-directed learning is the most beneficial.
5. Establish, with their help, methods of self-evaluation. Set up a checklist.

6. Involve them not only in content aims but also in classroom order, organization, and discipline. A "Deportment List" made by students is a sure way of getting their cooperation in class management.

E. Identify your content area (Level B)

1. Discuss the term "communications."
2. Differentiate between the work in regular English classes or in reading courses. (If this guide is used as an adjunct to a regular English class, make this concept clear for the units.)
3. Determine what the communications skills are: listening, speaking, reading, writing.
4. Impress pupils with the important, fundamental need for each skill.
5. Have them list how communication skills are needed in such areas as entertainment or a vocation.

F. Establish the sender-receiver concept (Level C)

1. The three essentials are: sender, message, receiver. Readers receive messages from writers. Listeners receive messages from speakers.
2. Messages may be signaled by gestures.
3. Sender and receiver must have an agreed-upon meaning: the thumb gesture of a hitch-hiker or a baseball umpire are examples.
4. Check on what careers require gestures most.

G. Have reachable goals (Level A)

1. Have pupils help set up aims for each unit or segment.
2. Have clear objectives, specific and measurable.
3. Help pupils see goals in terms of the activities that accompany each one.
4. If, in spite of everything, goals were not attained, frankly reassess why they were not. Make a fresh start and benefit by that error.
5. Use uncomplicated approaches in all lessons.

H. Relate this course to other content (Level B)

1. Establish the concept that communication is basic to every relationship.
2. Use examples and problems from student textbooks whenever possible.
3. Credit work from other classes which may be pertinent.

4. Work with teachers of other subjects to correlate ideas and activities.
5. Use school and community activities as a means of establishing aims and procedures.
6. Make "the present" as relevant as the future.

I. Use role-playing ideas
(Level C)

1. Use role playing to establish concepts in any area.
2. Vary role playing to include charades, auditions, interviews, silent or oral commercials, and skits.
3. In interviews, exchange roles of interviewer and interviewee.
4. Include the reluctant or shy pupil.
5. Expand students' knowledge of careers through role play and games.
6. Interpret slang through role playing.
7. Through role playing, interest students in cooperation rather than hostility.

J. Work with mass media
(Level A)

1. Define media and discuss examples.
2. Develop the concept of the human senses as the key to understanding. In your discussions, include the printed word (sight), radio (sound), television (sight and sound) and motion pictures (sight and sound).
3. Use newspapers and magazines as sources for learning; make specific assignments which make use of radio and television; have students write for each medium.
4. Discuss the impact of media on public life, emotions, and standards of living.

K. Compile lists of
communications needs
(Level B)

1. Use this activity as a part of setting goals and as a checklist in evaluating learning. Pupils can make separate lists and/or consolidate lists.
2. Have them include activities they engage in now as well as hopes for the future.
3. Expand their vicarious experience into areas they know little about:
   a. Space and related careers.
   b. Oceanography and related careers.
4. Develop and use these checklists as a motivating element as lessons proceed.

L. Include pupil-and-teacher evaluation (Level C)

1. Set up your own checklist.
2. Have pupils do the same from their point of view according to their learning aims.
3. If evaluation results are good, check to see if they could be better. If not, find out why.
4. Check to see if results are measurable in any way—perhaps in terms of better work habits, the desire to improve, increased understanding, or presenting more usable facts or ideas.
5. Have pupils answer such questions as "How would you grade this if you were the boss?"

Listening Objectives and Activities

**To Follow Directions
(Level A)**

1. Give oral instructions on preparing papers: margins, name, date, skip a line, put an X where you would a paragraph. Ask students to compare their work with a longhand model on the chalkboard or overhead projector.
2. Divide the class into teams. Give directions as in "Simon Says." Declare the winners, who will be the best listeners.
3. Help pupils role play such situations as:
   a. Tell a new boy on the block how to get to school. Have the new boy repeat the directions.
   b. You are a guide in school. Direct visitors to the library, cafeteria, or elsewhere.

**To Follow Directions
(Level B)**

1. Give a series of instructions which will result in a geometric figure if followed exactly. For example: "Place your pencil point in the center of the paper. Draw a 2-inch line toward the top of your paper. Stop. Start a new line from where your pencil point has stopped, going 2 inches to the left. Stop. Make a similar line going down 2 inches. Stop. Now make the line go right 2 inches. Do you have a square?" Compose other instructions like these.
2. Role play: Man on the street asks way to bus station. Repeat directions.
3. Tape an explanation of how to make or do something. Have pupils take turns repeating it step by step or in entirety.

4. Have pupils think of and work out other role-playing situations such as these.

To Follow Directions
(Level C)

1. Give each pupil a game, puzzle, or teacher-made kit. Give oral directions to complete.
2. Provide each pupil with an envelope containing printed strips. Give oral instructions as to how they should be arranged. If correct, a story is put together in correct sequence.
3. Play the "Echo Game": "Look in the cabinet and get 5 pencils, 9 notebooks, a box of rubber bands, and a handful of paper clips." The pupil should repeat this. Simplify or make more difficult as needed.

To Learn Facts (Level A)

1. Use any Listen and Read tape. Make the primary aim the learning of predetermined facts.
2. Use the "lead" paragraph of news stories to check listening for facts. Pupils may bring in clippings.
3. Prepare a tape containing facts about your school. Pupils tell how many different facts; ask a question to elicit the number of facts given on tape.

To Learn Facts (Level B)

1. Read short selections from the students' own science or social studies texts. Check this listening skill with questions.
2. Use radio and television in the classroom and for home assignments. Have pupils listen to information-type programs or watch the educational channel (if you have one in your city). Their follow-up discussions can be done on an individual, group, or panel basis.

To Learn Facts (Level C)

1. Have several pupils read to the class:
   a. notes from other classes
   b. home assignments
   c. book reports
Assign other pupils to discuss briefly, review, or evaluate what they heard. Continue this objective in other areas needing recall.

Specific Objectives in Listening

To follow directions
To learn facts
To improve habits of concentration
To differentiate between hearing and listening
To increase awareness of listening needs in daily relationships
To identify sounds
To discriminate between sounds
To appreciate sounds in context
To evaluate propriety of language and speech
To discriminate between varying intonations, voice quality, stress, or emphasis
To differentiate between main points and details
To differentiate between fact and opinion
To judge critically
To interpret ideas according to a speaker's background
To organize ideas (classifying; predicting; recognizing cause and effect; recognizing and establishing sequence)

Bibliography A: General Literature for the Student

Abrahams, Peter. *Tell Freedom.* London: Allen & Unwin, 1954.

Achebe, Chinua. *Things Fall Apart.* New York: Fawcett World, 1970.

Alegria, Ricardo E. *The Three Wishes: A Collection of Puerto Rican Folktales.* Translated by Elizabeth Culbert. New York: Harcourt Brace Jovanovich, 1969.

Anderson, Marian. *My Lord, What a Morning.* New York: Viking Press, 1956.

Baldwin, James. *Blues for Mr. Charlie.* New York: Dial Press, 1964.

———. *Go Tell It on the Mountain.* New York: Dell Publishing Co., 1970.

———. *Notes of a Native Son.* New York: Bantam Books, 1971.

Ball, Charles. *Slavery in the United States: A Narrative of the Life and Adventures of Charles Ball, A Black Man.* Detroit: Negro History Press, 1970. Originally published in 1836.

Bambara, Toni C., ed. *Tales and Stories for Black Folks.* New York: Doubleday & Co., 1971.

Beckett, Samuel. *Waiting for Godot.* New York: Grove Press, 1966.

Bellow, Saul. *Herzog.* New York: Viking Press, 1967.

Bennett, Lerone, Jr. *What Matter of Man: A Biography of Martin Luther King, Jr., 1929–1968.* Chicago: Johnson Publishing Co., 1964.

Bonham, Frank, *Durango Street.* New York: E. P. Dutton & Co., 1965.

Bontemps, Arna. "A Summer Tragedy." In *The Best Short Stories by Negro Writers,* edited by Langston Hughes. Boston: Little, Brown & Co., 1967.

Borland, Hal. *When the Legends Die.* Philadelphia: J. B. Lippincott Co., 1963.

Bradford, Sarah. *Harriet Tubman, The Moses of Her People.* New York: Corinth Books, 1961.

Braithewaite, E. R. *To Sir, With Love.* Englewood Cliffs, N.J.: Prentice-Hall, 1959.

Brooks, Charlotte K., ed. *The Outnumbered: Stories, Essays and Poems about Minority Groups.* New York: Delacorte Press, 1967.

Brooks, Charlotte K., and Trout, L., eds. *I've Got a Name.* New York: Holt, Rinehart & Winston, 1968.

Brown, W. W. *Narrative of William Wells Brown, A Fugitive Slave.* Westport, Conn.: Negro University Press, 1847.

Brutus, Dennis. *Letters to Martha.* London: Heinemann Books, 1969.

Buck, Pearl. *Fourteen Stories.* New York: John Day Company, 1961.

———. *Letter from Peking.* New York: Pocket Books, 1969.

————. *My Several Worlds.* New York: John Day Company, 1954.

Campbell, Joseph. *The Hero with a Thousand Faces.* New York: Pantheon Books, 1961.

Camus, Albert. *The Stranger.* Translated by Gilbert Stuart. New York: Random House. Reprint of 1946 edition.

Cather, Willa. *My Ántonia.* Boston: Houghton Mifflin Co.

Cavanna, Betty. *Jenny Kimura.* New York: William Morrow & Co.

Chang, Isabelle C. *Tales From Old China.* New York: Random House.

Chapman, Abraham, ed. *Steal Away; Stories of the Runaway Slaves.* New York: Praeger, 1971.

Chekhov, Anton. *The Three Sisters.* New York: Avon Books, 1965.

Colman, Hila. *The Girl from Puerto Rico.* New York: Dell Publishing Co., 1968.

Conrad, Earl. *Harriet Tubman.* New York: Paul S. Eriksson, 1970.

Dave-Danquah, Mabel. "Anticipation." In *An African Treasury,* edited by Langston Hughes. New York: Pyramid Publications, 1960.

Davis, Sammy, Jr. *Yes, I Can.* New York: Farrar, Straus & Giroux, 1965.

DeAngulo, Jaime. *Indian Tales.* New York: Hill & Wang, 1962.

Douglass, Frederick. *The Life and Times of Frederick Douglass: The Complete Autobiography.* New York: Macmillan Co., 1962.

Duberman, Martin. *In White America.* Boston: Houghton Mifflin Co., 1964.

Dunbar, Paul. "The Party." In *American Negro Poetry,* edited by Arna Bontemps. New York: Hill & Wang, 1963.

Ekwens, Cyprian. *Jagua Nana.* New York: Fawcett World, 1969.

Elder, Lonne. *Ceremonies in Dark Old Men.* New York: Farrar, Straus & Giroux, 1969.

Ellison, Ralph. *The Invisible Man.* New York: Modern Library, 1963.

Equiano, Olaudah. *The Life of Olaudah Equiano, Or, Gustavus Vassa, the African.* New York: Humanities Press, 1969. Originally published in 1789.

Ewers, Carolyn. *Long Journey: A Biography of Sidney Poitier.* New York: New American Library, 1969.

Felsen, Henry G. *Hot Rod.* New York: AMSCO School Publications, 1970.

Foner, Philip, S. *Frederick Douglass: A Biography.* New York: Citadel Press, 1969.

Fromm, Erich. *The Art of Loving: An Enquiry into the Nature of Love.* New York: Harper & Row, Publishers, 1956.

Gardner, Mona. "Dinner Party." In *At Your Own Risk,* edited by Charlotte K. Brooks. New York: Holt, Rinehart & Winston, 1968.

Gibson, Althea, with Ed Fitzerald. *I Always Wanted to Be Somebody.* New York: Harper & Row, Publishers, 1968.

Goodrich, Frances, and Hackett, Albert, eds. *The Diary of Anne Frank.* New York: Random House.

Graham, Shirley. *There Was Once a Slave: The Heroic Story of Frederick Douglass.* New York: Julian Messner, 1947.

Greene, James A. *Wendell Phillips: A Biography.* New York: International Publishers Co.

Gregory, Dick. *Nigger: An Autobiography.* Edited by Robert Lipsyte. New York: E. P. Dutton & Co., 1964.

Handed, Left, and Dyk, Walter. *Son of Old Man Hat: A Navaho Autobiography.* Lincoln: University of Nebraska Press, 1967.

Handy, W. C. *Father of the Blues.* New York: Macmillan Co., 1970.

Hansberry, Lorraine. *A Raisin in the Sun.* New York: New American Library, 1961.
_____. *The Sign in Sidney Brustein's Window.* New York: Random House, 1965.
_____. *To Be Young, Gifted and Black.* Adapted by Robert Nemiraf. Englewood Cliffs, N.J.: Prentice-Hall, 1969.
Hart, Moss. *Act One.* New York: Ballantine Books, 1970.
Hinton, S. E. *The Outsiders.* New York: Dell Publishing Co.. Reprint of 1967 editon.
Hughes, Langston. *Five Plays by Langston Hughes.* Edited by Webster Smalley. (Bloomington: Indiana University Press, 1968.) Includes *Mulatto; Soul Gone Home; Little Ham; Simply Heavenly; Tambourines to Glory.*
_____. *"I, Too, Sing America."* In *Selected Poems by Langston Hughes.* New York: Alfred A. Knopf, 1926.
_____. "Mother to Son." In *The Poetry of the Negro, 1946–1949.* Edited by Langston Hughes and Arna Bontemps. Garden City, N.Y.: Doubleday & Co., 1956.
Hurston, Zora N. "The Gilded Six-Bits." In *The Best Short Stories by Negro Writers,* edited by Langston Hughes. Boston: Little, Brown & Co., 1967.
Ibsen, Henrik. *The Doll's House.* Edited by Harry Shefter. New York: Washington Square Press, 1968.
Inouye, Daniel K., and Elliott, Lawrence. *Journey to Washington.* Englewood Cliffs, N.J.: Prentice-Hall, 1967.
Ionesco, Eugene. *Rhinoceros.* New York: Holt, Rinehart & Winston, 1961.
Irving, Washington. *The Legend of Sleepy Hollow and Other Stories.* New York: Airmont Publishing Co., 1964.
Johnson, Lady Bird. *White House Diary.* New York: Holt, Rinehart & Winston, 1970.
Jones, LeRoi. *The Dutchman.* New York: Apollo Editions, 1966.
Joyce, James. *The Portrait of the Artist as a Young Man.* Edited by Richard Ellmann. New York: Viking Press.
Kafka, Franz. *The Penal Colony: Stories & Short Pieces Including The Metamorphosis.* New York: Schocken Books, 1948.
_____. *The Trial.* New York: Random House, 1969.
Kaufman, Bel. *Up the Down Staircase.* Englewood Cliffs, N.J.: Prentice-Hall, 1964.
Knowles, John. *A Separate Peace.* New York: Dell Publishing Co. Reprint of 1960 edition.
Koestler, Arthur. *Darkness at Noon.* New York: Bantam Books, 1970.
Kosinski, Jerzy. *The Painted Bird.* New York: Pocket Books, 1970.
Laluah, Aqua. "The Serving Girl." In *An African Treasury,* edited by Langston Hughes. New York: Pyramid Publications, 1960.
Laye, Camara. *The Dark Child.* New York: Farrar, Straus & Giroux, 1970.
Lewis, Oscar. *La Vida.* New York: Random House, 1966.
_____. *The Children of Sanchez.* New York: Random House.
Lurie, Nancy O., ed. *Mountain Wolf Woman, Sister of Crashing Thunder: The Autobiography of a Winnebago Indian.* Ann Arbor: University of Michigan Press, 1961.
Malcolm X and Alex Haley. *The Autobiography of Malcolm X.* New York: Grove Press, 1965.
Markandaya, Kamala. *Nectar in a Sieve.* New York: New American Library. Reprint of 1955 edition.
Miller, Warren. *The Cool World.* New York: Fawcett World, 1969.
Moody, Anne. *Coming of Age in Mississippi.* New York: Dell Publishing Co., 1970.

Mphahlele, Ezekial. "Mrs. Plum." In *African Short Stories*, edited by C. R. Larson. New York: World Publishing Co., 1969.

Naylor, Phyllis. *Dark Side of the Moon*. Philadelphia: Fortress Press, 1969.

Nicol, Abiose. "Life Is Sweet at Kumansenu." In *Black Africa*, edited by Wells Stevenson. New York: Harcourt Brace Jovanovich, 1970.

———. "The Truly Married Woman." In *African Short Stories*. Suffolk, Eng.: Chaucer Press, 1969.

Ntantola, Phyllis. "The Widows of the Reserves." In *An African Treasury*, edited by Langston Hughes. New York: Pyramid Publications, 1960.

Nwapa, Flora. *Ehuru*. London: Heinemann Books, 1966.

O'Neill, Eugene. *The Emperor Jones*. New York: Modern Library,

Ousmane, Sembene. "Black Girl." In *African Short Stories*, edited by C. S. Larson. New York: World Publishing Co., 1969.

Paige, LeRoy (Satchel), and Lipman, David. *Maybe I'll Pitch Forever*. Garden City, N.Y.: Doubleday & Co., 1962.

Parks, Gordon. *A Choice of Weapons*. New York: Noble & Noble, 1968.

———. *The Learning Tree*. New York: Fawcett World, 1970.

Paton, Alan. *Cry, the Beloved Country*. New York: Charles Scribner's, 1948.

P'Bitek, Okot. *Son of Lawino*. New York: World Publishing Co., 1969.

Petry, Ann. *The Street*. Boston: Houghton Mifflin Co.

Pinter, Harold. *Two Plays, Including The Birthday Party; The Room*. New York: Grove Press, 1961.

Potok, Chaim. *The Chosen*. New York: Fawcett World, 1968.

Redding, Saunders. *The Lonesome Road: The Story of the Negro in America*. Garden City, N.Y.: Doubleday & Co.

Rodin, Paul, ed. *African Folktales*. Princeton, N.J.: Princeton University Press, 1952.

Roethke, Theodore. "My Papa's Waltz," In *Collected Poems*. Garden City, N.Y.: Doubleday & Co., 1966.

Ross, Leonard. "Cemetery Path." In *At Your Own Risk*, edited by Charlotte K. Brooks. New York: Holt, Rinehart & Winston, 1968.

Russell, Bill, as told to William McSweeney. *Go Up for Glory*. New York: Noble & Noble, 1968.

Rutherford, Peggy, ed. *African Voices*. New York: Grosset & Dunlap, 1969.

Salinger, J. D. *Catcher in the Rye*. New York: Bantam Books, 1970.

Saroyan, William. *The Human Comedy*. New York: Dell Publishing Co. Reprint of 1944 edition.

Sartre, Jean-Paul. *No Exit & Three Other Plays*. New York: Random House.

Selormey, Francis. *The Narrow Path*. London: Heinemann Books, 1969.

Shaw, George Bernard. *Pygmalion*. Baltimore: Penguin Books.

Sherlock, Philip K. *The Iguana's Tail: Crick Crack Stories from the Caribbean*. New York: Thomas Y. Crowell, 1969.

Shotwell, Louisa R. *Roosevelt Grady*. New York: Grosset & Dunlap, 1964.

Sillitoe, Alan. *Loneliness of the Long-Distance Runner*. New York: Alfred A. Knopf, 1960.

Steichen, Edward. *The Family of Man*. New York: Simon & Schuster, 1955.

Stuart, Jesse. *God's Oddling*. New York: McGraw-Hill Book Co., 1960.

Sutherland, Efua. "New Life at Kyerefaso." In *An African Treasury,* edited by Langston Hughes. New York: Pyramid Publications, 1960.

Thomas, Piri. *Down These Mean Streets.* New York: New American Library, 1971.

Toomer, Jean. *Cane.* New York: Harper & Row, Publishers, 1968.

Tutolo, Amos. *The Brave African Huntress.* New York: Grove Press, 1953.

Twain, Mark. *Huckleberry Finn.* New York: Dodd, Mead & Co., 1953.

Updike, John. *Rabbit, Run.* New York: Fawcett World, 1970.

Walker, Margaret. *Jubilee.* Boston: Houghton Mifflin Co., 1966.

Waters, Ethel. *His Eye Is on the Sparrow.* Garden City, N.Y.: Doubleday & Co., 1951.

Weiner, Sandra. *It's Wings That Makes Birds Fly.* New York: Pantheon Books, 1968.

Williams, Tennessee. *A Streetcar Named Desire.* New York: New Directions Publishing Corp., 1947.

————. *The Glass Menagerie.* New York: New Directions Publishing Corp.

Wright, Richard. *Black Boy.* New York: Harper & Row, Publishers, 1945.

Bibliography B: Professional Literature for the Teacher

Arnez, N. L. "Liberal Education for Junior High School Students in a Culturally Limited Area." *Journal of Negro Education* 33 (1964): 436–40.

Brooks, Charlotte K. "Some Approaches to Teaching Standard English as a Second Language." *Elementary English* 41 (1964): 728–33.

Bruner, Jerome S. *Toward a Theory of Instruction.* Cambridge, Mass: Harvard University Press, 1966.

Burns, Paul Clay, and Schell, Leo M. *Elementary School Language Arts: Selected Readings.* Chicago: Rand McNally & Co., 1969.

Conant, James B. *Adventure in Human Relations.* New York: McGraw-Hill, 1961.

Epstein, Jason. Articles on the New York City Schools. *The New York Review of Books,* 6 June 1968, 10 October 1968, 21 November 1968, 13 March 1969.

Fader, Daniel, and McNeil, Elton B. *Hooked on Books: Program and Proof.* New York: Berkley Publishing Corp., 1968.

Featherstone, Joseph. "The Primary School Revolution in Britain." *The New Republic,* 10 August 1967, 2 September 1967, 9 September 1967.

Friedenberg, Edgar. *The Vanishing Adolescent.* New York: Dell Publishing Co., 1959.

Gibbons, Maurice. *Individualized Instruction.* New York: Bureau of Publications, Teachers College Press, Columbia University, 1971.

Grier, William H., and Cobbs, Price M. *Black Rage.* New York: Bantam Books, 1969.

Guth, Hans P. *English Today and Tomorrow.* Englewood Cliffs, N.J.: Prentice-Hall, 1964.

Havighurst, Robert J. "The Educationally Difficult Student: What the Schools Can Do." *Bulletin of the National Association of Secondary-School Principals* 49 (1965): 110–27.

Hentoff, Nat. *Our Children Are Dying.* New York: Viking Press, 1966.

Herndon, James. *The Way It Spozed to Be.* New York: Simon & Schuster, 1968.

Holsinger, Rosemary; Jordan, Camille; and Levenson, Leon. *The Creative Encounter.* Glenview, Ill.: Scott, Foresman & Co., 1971.

Holt, John. *How Children Fail.* New York: Pitman Publishing Corp., 1968.

Holt, John. *How Children Learn.* New York: Pitman Publishing Corp., 1969.

Jewett, Arno; Mersand, Joseph; and Gunderson, Doris V. *Improving English Skills of Culturally Different Youth in Large Cities.* U.S. Department of Health, Education and Welfare, Office of Education, Bulletin 1964, no. 5. Washington, D.C.: Government Printing Office, 1964.

Kohl, Herbert R. *36 Children*. New York: New American Library, 1967.

Kozol, Jonathan. *Death at an Early Age*. Boston: Houghton Mifflin Co., 1967.

Lawler, Marcella R., ed. *Strategies for Planned Curricular Innovation*. New York: Columbia University Press, 1970.

Loban, Walter; Ryan, Margaret; and Squire, James. *Teaching Language and Literature*. New York: Harcourt Brace Jovanovich, 1969.

Malstrom, Jean. *Language in Society*. New York: Hayden Book Co., 1965.

Marin, Peter. "The Open Truth and Fiery Vehemence of Youth" and "The Schools." *The Center Magazine,* January 1969.

Maxwell, John, and Tovatt, Anthony, eds. *On Writing Behavioral Objectives for English*. Commission of the English Curriculum, National Council of Teachers of English, 1970.

Moffett, James. *A Student-Centered Language Arts Curriculum*. Grades K–13: A Handbook for Teachers. Boston: Houghton Mifflin Co., 1968.

Neill, A. S. *Summerhill*. New York: Hart Publishing Co., 1960.

Passow, A. Harry, ed. *Education in Depressed Areas*. New York: Bureau of Publications, Teachers College, Columbia University, 1963.

Postman, Neil, and Weingartner, Charles. *Teaching as a Subversive Activity*. New York: Delacorte Press, 1969.

Probst, Robert. In *High School: The Process and the Place,* edited by Ruth Weinstock. New York: Educational Facilities Laboratories, 1972.

Riessman, Frank, and Riessman, Hannah A. "Big-City School: Problems and Prospects; Teachers of the Poor." *PTA Magazine* 59 (1964): 12–14.

Rukeyser, Muriel. "Effort at Speech between Two People." *A Treasury of Great Poems, English and American,* vol. II, rev. and annotated by Louis Untermeyer. New York: Simon & Schuster, 1942.

Sauer, Edwin H. *English in the Secondary School*. New York: Holt, Rinehart & Winston, 1961.

Shuy, Roger W. *American Dialects*. Sponsored by NCTE Commission of the English Language. Champaign, Ill.: National Council of Teachers of English, 1967.

Silberman, Charles. *Crisis in the Classroom*. New York: Random House, 1970.

Textbook Series for the Uninvolved Learner: Gateway Series (New York: Macmillan Co.); Impact Series (New York: Holt, Rinehart & Winston); Crossroads Series (New York: Noble and Noble Publishers).

Weber, Julia. *My Country School Diary*. New York: Dell Publishing Co., 1969.

Index